Every Child Matters
A New Role for SENCOs

Also available:

How to Create the Inclusive Classroom: Removing barriers to learning
Rita Cheminais 1 84312 240 5

Closing the Inclusion Gap: Special and mainstream schools working partnership
Rita Cheminais 1 84312 085 2

Meeting SEN in the Curriculum: English
Tim Hurst 1 84312 157 3

Meeting SEN in the Curriculum: Maths
Brian Sharp 1 84312 158 1

Meeting SEN in the Curriculum: Citizenship
Alan Combes 1 84312 169 7

Meeting SEN in the Curriculum: Religious Education
Dilwyn Hunt 184312 167 0

Meeting SEN in the Curriculum: History
Richard Harris and Ian Luff 1 84312 163 8

Meeting SEN in the Curriculum: Geography
Diane Swift 1 84312 162 X

Meeting SEN in the Curriculum: Design and Technology
Louise T. Davies 1 84312 166 2

Meeting SEN in the Curriculum: Art
Kim Earle and Gill Curry 1 84312 161 1

Meeting SEN in the Curriculum: PE/Sports
Crispin Andrews 1 84312 164 6

Meeting SEN in the Curriculum: Modern Foreign Languages
Sally McKeown 1 84312 165 4

Meeting SEN in the Curriculum: Music
Victoria Jaquiss and Diane Paterson 1 84312 168 9

Meeting SEN in the Curriculum: ICT
Michael North and Sally McKeown 1 84312 160 3

Meeting SEN in the Curriculum: Science
Carol Holden and Andy Cooke 1 84312 159 X

Every Child Matters
A New Role for SENCOs

RITA CHEMINAIS

 David Fulton Publishers

David Fulton Publishers Ltd
The Chiswick Centre, 414 Chiswick High Road, London W4 5TF

www.fultonpublishers.co.uk

David Fulton Publishers is a division of Granada Learning Limited, part of ITV plc.

British Library Cataloguing in Publication Data
A catalogue record for this book is available from the British Library.

ISBN: 1 84312 406 8

10 9 8 7 6 5 4 3 2 1

Typeset by RefineCatch, Bungay, Suffolk
Printed and bound in Great Britain

Contents

Contents of CD

- The government's programme of change
- *Every Child Matters* – five outcomes for children and young people
- Implications of *Every Child Matters* for the SENCO role
- Example of a school development plan to implement *Every Child Matters*
- *Removing Barriers to Achievement* – the government's strategy for SEN
- Audit for new SENCO role
- At-a-glance summary of the National Service Framework standards for children, young people and maternity services
- The division of responsibilities between schools and local authorities for SEN monitoring
- Additional indicators for schools – for the inclusion of SEN pupils
- Model school SEN profile
- Self-evaluation for accounting for annual SEN budget amounts
- School evaluation of impact/outcomes of SEN provision
- Model framework for an SEN provision map (Foundation Stage/Primary)
- Model framework for an SEN provision map (Secondary phase)
- Evaluating the impact of additional SEN provision on outcomes for SEN pupils
- OFSTED criteria for self-evaluation of SEN and inclusion
- SEN monitoring and evaluation cycle for schools
- School self-evaluation framework for SEN and *Every Child Matters* outcomes for children and young people
- Summary of recommendations related to reducing SEN bureaucracy
- A user-friendly lesson observation schedule aligned with ECM outcomes

Acknowledgements

Thanks are due to colleagues within the Inclusion and School Improvement Service (ISIS) in Cheshire Local Authority, who through their constant support have encouraged me to continue to write books on inclusion and special educational needs. While the school self-evaluation framework for SEN and *Every Child Matters*, which is included on the CD, has been adopted for use within Cheshire Local Authority, this framework was written and produced by myself as the original author in its current format. I consider it to be a great privilege to be able to share my work not only within my own local authority, but also with a wider national audience of SENCOs.

Special thanks go to:

Linda Brown, County Manager for ISIS in Cheshire, for her belief in my ideas and vision;

Philip Eastwood, my critical friend and Advanced Skills Teacher for Initial Teacher Training at St Mary and St Paul's CofE Primary School in Knowsley, for his personal encouragement and for inspiring me to keep writing;

Zita McCormick, SEN Team Leader in Hertfordshire Children's Services, for putting my ideas on inclusion into practice;

Sandy Thomas, for giving up her own time outside work to help me improve my ICT skills in order to present charts correctly;

all the SENCOs who have heard me speak nationally, and those with whom I work closely in Cheshire, for their enthusiasm and commitment to raising standards for children with SEN in mainstream and special schools; and

last, but not least, Linda Evans, my commissioning editor with David Fulton Publishers, for her invaluable advice, guidance and enthusiasm for my ideas.

While every effort has been made to acknowledge sources throughout the book, such is the range of aspects covered that I may have unintentionally omitted to mention their origin. If so, I offer my apologies to all concerned.

This book is dedicated to my mother, whose support, encouragement and patient quietness has been much appreciated during the writing of this book.

Abbreviations

AEN	additional educational needs
ASD	autistic spectrum disorder
AST	advanced skills teacher
AWPU	age-weighted pupil unit
BESD	Behavioural, emotional and social development
CAF	Common Assessment Framework
CAMHS	Child and Adolescent Mental Health Service
CPD	continuing professional development
DfES	Department for Education and Skills
DoH	Department of Health
DRC	Disability Rights Commission
EAL	English as an additional language
EBD	emotional and behavioural difficulties
ECM	*Every Child Matters*
EiC	Excellence in Cities
FE	further education
FFT	Fischer Family Trust
FS	Foundation stage
FSM	free school meals
FTE	full-time equivalent
GP	general practitioner
HE	higher education
HLTA	higher level teaching assistant
HMI	Her Majesty's Inspector
IBP	individual behaviour plan
ICT	information and communication technology
IEP	Individual Education Plan
INCO	inclusion co-ordinator
INSET	in-service education and training
ITT	initial teacher training
KS	key stage
LA	local authority
LEA	local education authority
LIG	Leadership Incentive Grant
LMS	local management of schools
LSA	learning support assistant
LSC	Learning Skills Council
MLD	moderate learning difficulties

NC	National Curriculum
NCSL	National College for School Leadership
NGfL	National Grid for Learning
NHS	National Health Service
NQT	newly qualified teacher
NRwS	New Relationship with Schools
NSF	National Service Framework
NUT	National Union of Teachers
OECD	Organisation for Economic Co-operation and Development
OFSTED	Office for Standards in Education
PANDA	Performance and Assessment Report
PAT	Pupil Achievement Tracker
PIVATS	Performance Indicators for Value Added Target Setting
PLASC	Pupil Level Annual School Census
PMT	Performance Management Threshold
PPA	planning, preparation and assessment
PSD	personal and social development
PSHE	Personal, Social and Health Education
PST	public sector team
QCA	Qualifications and Curriculum Authority
QTS	qualified teacher status
RBA	*Removing Barriers to Achievement*
RE	religious education
RGI	Regulatory Impact Unit
SDP	school development plan
SEF	self-evaluation form
SEN	special educational needs
SENCO	Special Educational Needs Co-ordinator
SEND	Special Educational Needs Disability Division
SENDA	Special Educational Needs and Disability Act
SENDIST	Special Educational Needs and Disability Tribunal
SIP	school improvement partner
SLCN	speech, language and communication needs
SMT	senior management team
SpLD	specific learning difficulties
SSC	Sector Skills Council
TA	teaching assistant
TLC	Transforming Learning Communities
TTA	Teacher Training Agency
UK	United Kingdom
USA	United States of America

The Aim of this Book

The aim of this book is to enable senior managers and SENCOs in early years settings, primary and secondary schools to know:

- what their role and expectations are in the light of the government's programme for change;
- how to plan and prepare for the implementation of *Every Child Matters*, the Children Act 2004 and the government's strategy for SEN;
- how to develop a new relationship with schools in raising standards in SEN and inclusion;
- how best to transform inclusive learning communities in order to build responsive schools for the future;
- how to quality-assure SEN policy and provision in partnership, through co-ordinated monitoring and school self-evaluation, aligned to the new OFSTED inspections and the five key outcomes of *Every Child Matters*;
- how to reduce bureaucracy in special educational needs and respond to the recommended new ways of working.

Who the book is for:

- head teachers and other senior managers in mainstream and special schools;
- SEN co-ordinators (SENCOs), Inclusion co-ordinators (INCOs), inclusion managers, learning managers, teaching and learning co-ordinators, key stage learning leaders, advanced skills teachers for SEN and BESD;
- local authority officers, advisers, inspectors, educational psychologists and consultants working in Children's Services;
- health and social services professionals working with head teachers and SENCOs in the delivery of wraparound services and care in schools and children's centres;
- governors with responsibility for SEN, inclusion and safeguarding children;
- senior education lecturers in higher education.

How the format is designed to be used

The book and accompanying CD provide a resource that can be used:

- to act as a point of quick reference for senior managers and SENCOs in schools, and to local authority children's services professionals working with children, young people and families;
- to inform more responsive localised SEN and inclusion policy and provision;
- to enable pages to be photocopied for developmental purposes, within the purchasing institution or service; and
- to allow readers to download and customise templates from the CD.

Introduction

Transforming learning communities

Every Child Matters marks a significant commitment to the nurturing and education of the whole child through effective inter-agency and community support. It represents a core legislative framework within the Children Act 2004 that works in synergy with other key government strategies to drive forward a holistic approach to learning and development. These strategies include: the Primary Strategy, the Secondary Strategy, the 14–19 Strategy, the Strategy for SEN, the Five Year Strategy, the Ten Year Strategy for Childcare, and Workforce Reform and Remodelling.

There are five outcomes for children and young people that are central to the government's programme of change for effective joined-up children's services:

- being healthy;
- staying safe;
- enjoying and achieving;
- making a positive contribution; and
- achieving economic wellbeing.

Children, young people and families should be able to make informed decisions about the support that they need in the knowledge that organisations will listen to them and respond to their needs. This will result in high-quality universal services such as early years and childcare provision, personalised learning in schools and a wider range of opportunities and support for young people, including effective targeted and specialist services for children with disabilities and those looked after by local authorities, or engaging in offending anti-social behaviour.

SENCOs and senior managers in schools of the future will need to develop skills which enable them to manage SEN provision and inclusion policy in the context of 'dawn till dusk' extended full-service schools, providing 'wraparound' care and educational services for children, young people and families.

The government, in its Strategy for SEN, clearly sees SENCOs as having a major role to play in enabling and effecting change, whereby all teachers in mainstream schools will feel more confident and competent in delivering improvements for children with a diversity of special educational needs in the classroom:

> SENCOs play a pivotal role co-ordinating provision across the school and linking class and subject teachers with SEN specialists to improve the quality of teaching and learning. We want schools to see the SENCO as a key member of their senior leadership team; able to influence the development of policies for whole school improvement.
> (DfES 2004a: 3.14)

New role for SENCOs

Transforming learning communities through extended full-service schools, specialist schools, foundation partnerships and children's trusts will require SENCOs to be:

- lead professionals in SEN and inclusion;
- knowledgeable managers of personalised learning approaches;
- advisers to colleagues within schools and from other external services;
- solution assemblers and key members of the problem-solving School Change Team;
- advocates for children, young people, parents and carers;
- commissioning agents brokering and mobilising resources and services for children and young people with SEN and disabilities;
- change champions facilitating the learning and wellbeing of children and young people with a diversity of SEN;
- innovators of sustainable SEN developments in transformed learning communities;
- strategic managers and partners in Removing Barriers to Achievement;
- quality assurers for SEN policy and provision; and
- network partners, coaches and mentors in networked learning communities.

As schools adopt more of a multi-agency focus they will no longer be the sole site for, and provider of, learning, but instead, gateways to a network of learning opportunities and activities provided by other local schools, colleges, distance learning programmes, e-learning, and private companies. This new way of delivering educational provision links closely to the concept of personalised learning which enables children and young people to achieve the best they can through working in a way that suits them.

Services for children and young people will become far more user-centred and solution-focused and able to deliver improved personalised outcomes through participation. This will ensure users are active participants in the shaping, development and delivery of education and related services. Personalisation is about enabling producers and users to work together to create the services that best meet and respond to local needs.

The government's strategy for SEN emphasises:

> All children have the right to a good education and the opportunity to fulfil their potential. All teachers should expect to teach children with special educational needs and all schools should play their part in educating children from the local community, whatever their background or ability. (DfES 2004a: Introduction)

Every Child Matters: Change for Children in Schools identifies that pupil performance and wellbeing go hand-in-hand. Children and young people cannot learn if they do not feel safe or if health problems create barriers. *Every Child Matters* also strongly supports the principle of personalisation and acknowledges the work done by schools already in this area by:

- encouraging schools to offer a range of extended services that help pupils engage and achieve, and building stronger relationships with parents and the wider community; and
- supporting closer working between universal services like schools and specialist services (health, social services) to promote children's welfare, to safeguard children from abuse and neglect, so that children with additional needs can be identified earlier and supported effectively. (DfES 2004m: 1)

It is vital that SENCOs are provided with quality leadership training to meet the demands of their increasingly pivotal role in schools. SENCOs continually find themselves managing across the entire range of personnel in a school, negotiating with and influencing colleagues from the head teacher to the least experienced member of staff. They also liaise regularly with parents, carers and a range of professionals from outside agencies to ensure children and young people's needs are met, and that the five outcomes of *Every Child Matters* are achieved. They are also likely to be at the forefront of innovative inclusive classroom practice in terms of facilitating and enhancing pupils' learning and wellbeing.

1

Challenge, Change and New Opportunities for SENCOs

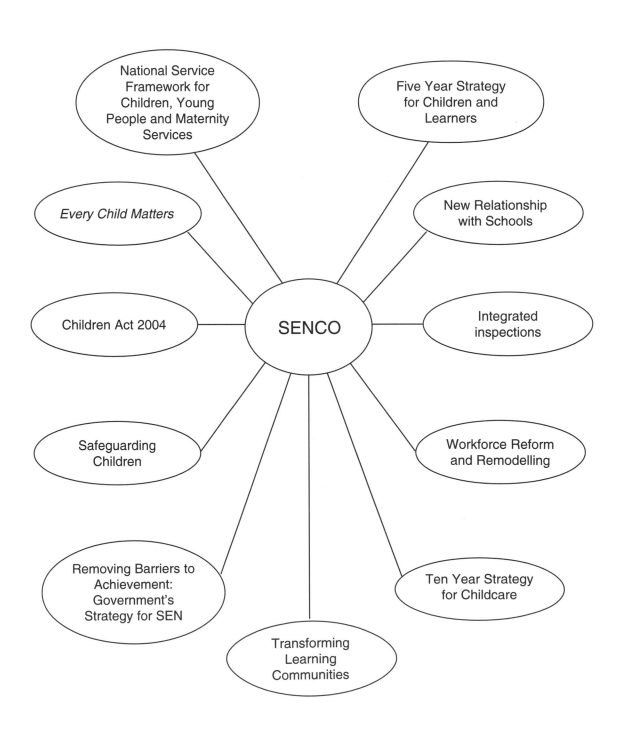

The challenge for SENCOs

The role of SENCO has expanded considerably in recent years in both the primary and secondary phases of education, owing to the increased number of new central government initiatives and administrative requirements generated by local authorities. Unfortunately, the amount of support and time available for SENCOs during the school day to meet these increasing demands has failed to keep pace with this expansion of role.

So many new initiatives, and the additional expectations they have generated (with very little support from outside agencies), makes the discharge of the majority of SENCOs' responsibilities an unattainable and unrealistic goal for one person alone. Some larger schools have moved towards dividing the role between two staff; for example: SENCO and Assistant SENCO; SENCO and INCO or learning manager, in order to make it more manageable and realistic.

External agencies are generally too thinly spread and, once accessed, the support from educational psychologists or learning support services has largely been focused on advice, guidance, observations and meetings, and less on direct work with children and young people. This has not stopped SENCOs being overburdened with repetitious bureaucratic application systems to access these different agencies.

Inadequate funding to schools for SEN provision has often meant that SENCOs have had insufficient non-contact time to do their job. SENCOs often have additional responsibilities; in smaller primary schools, for example, they may be subject leader, child protection officers, deputy head teachers, head teachers, or full-time classroom teachers. Other barriers cited by SENCOs as preventing them from obtaining sufficient non-contact time on a regular basis include:

- difficulties with obtaining supply cover;
- the need to cover for staff absence at short notice; and
- a lack of understanding among school staff of the demanding requirements of the post of SENCO.

Where SENCOs are experiencing a reduction in their non-contact time on a regular basis, due to covering classes for other subject leaders to obtain release time, or for absent colleagues, the recommendation is to ask the head teacher which areas of the SENCO role they should relinquish.

SENCOs are subject to high anxiety and stress levels, particularly when parents of pupils with SEN and disability start to pursue the tribunal course of action (SENDIST) for redress. The intrusion that the SEN Code of Practice paperwork already makes into SENCOs' family life and work–life balance is immense.

The SEN Bureaucracy Project (DfES/Cabinet Office Regulatory Impact Unit 2004) recommended that the governing body of the school should take the lead in examining the impact of changes and initiatives on the SENCO's ability to work effectively. The SEN governor, in particular, can help to facilitate and support a manageable workload for the SENCO. Problems of workload, role definition, lack of involvement in key aspects of school leadership and the low status of SEN provision in some schools continue to prevent the development of improved and innovative practice. This is in spite of the government's policy guidance that acknowledges the need to provide a more structured and supportive framework for SENCOs to operate within.

The NUT Survey (2004) on the impact of the SEN Code of Practice on SENCOs revealed a wide variation in the amount of weekly non-contact time allocated to enable them to carry out their specific responsibilities. On average, SENCOs receive between one and five hours of non-contact time per week. The wide variation in the amount of non-contact time allocated to

SENCOs is often related to the size of the school in which they work, the number of pupils with statements and the number of pupils at Action and Action Plus within the school. Protected non-contact time for SENCOs should be allocated on a more flexible basis in order to take account of the particularly busy times and pressure points in the SEN year – for example, more non-contact time should be allocated in September, mid-year around early February and at the end of the year in June and July, when SENCOs are preparing for transitions and new pupils joining the school.

OFSTED (2004a) acknowledged the valuable role of SENCOs in enabling the inclusion of SEN pupils in its report *Special Educational Needs and Disability: Towards Inclusive Schools*, which commented:

> Much effective work has been done by SENCOs to develop staff awareness through training and information about classroom strategies. (para. 28)

The new educational agenda of *Every Child Matters* increases considerably the responsibility and accountability placed on SENCOs. But senior managers in schools have a tendency to view SENCOs as managers of SEN departments and managers of SEN staff, rather than manager-leaders with strategic responsibilities. These responsibilities are about removing barriers to achievement for children and young people with a diversity of additional needs, throughout the learning community, which may go beyond the school and school hours. Many SENCOs are still working under conditions that counter their efforts to develop such a new leadership role.

The National College for School Leadership (NCSL) in the 'Leading from the Middle' enrichment programme for SENCOs, enables them to further improve their established managerial and leadership skills in order to become members of school senior leadership teams. The programme covers: leadership of innovation and change; knowledge and understanding of their role in leading teaching and learning; enhancing self-confidence and skills as team leaders; building team capacity through the efficient use of staff and resources; and active engagement in self-directed change in a blended learning environment.

New opportunities for SENCOs

In the current government's programme of change, the traditional role of the SENCO needs reconfiguring in order to meet the exciting and radical changes in schools that lie ahead over the next five to ten years.

Education reform, particularly in relation to extended full-service schools, requires SENCOs to become far more strategic in their leadership role, possibly transforming into the inclusion co-ordinator, inclusion manager or learning manager roles, as part of a networked learning community, which necessitates senior management status and usually aligns with the role of deputy head teacher or assistant head teacher.

This opportunity for strengthening the status of the SENCO in a school leads, undoubtedly, to a re-conceptualisation of their role, in order to meet the 'brave new world' and respond to the required 'blue sky' thinking. The model on p. 9 (Figure 1.1) exemplifies the SENCO's strategic management role in schools of the future.

SENCOs, along with head teachers, will become key strategic partners in shaping the pattern of local services for children, young people and families through Foundation Partnerships and other clustering arrangements. Plans for wraparound care – one-stop shops offering a range of universal services on school sites or within schools – will have huge implications for the role of the SENCO. This is because disadvantaged children (of whom a high number have special

Table 1.1 The government's Programme of Change

SCHOOL SELF-EVALUATION SEN POLICY AND PROVISION (OFSTED FRAMEWORK)

Effectiveness and efficiency of current SEN provision and related services, and what needs further improvement

Achievement and standards

Quality of provision

1. How well do SEN pupils achieve?
2. How effective is teaching, training and learning?
3. How well do programmes and activities meet the needs and interests of SEN pupils?
4. How well are SEN pupils guided and supported?

Leadership and management

5. How effective are leadership and management in raising achievement and supporting SEN pupils?

Judgements made on OFSTED criteria (1 Outstanding; 2 Good; 3 Satisfactory; 4 Inadequate).

LA SEN FUNDING FORMULA (ACCOUNTABILITY – INPUT/OUTCOMES)

- Delegating % AWPU as general funding designated to schools for SEN
- Formula funding on basis of prior attainment, FSM
- 'Top up' funding for pupils with severe and complex needs based on audit – level of need assessed against clear criteria

LA in partnership with schools:

- Monitor use of school SEN funding in supporting and raising achievements of SEN pupils, through scrutiny of school SEN provision map and annual SEN budget
- Demonstrate the impact and effect SEN funding delegated directly to schools has on SEN pupil outcomes (data analysis to identify value added rates of progress, trends and underachievement)
- Provide parents/carers with clear information about the progress and attainments of their child; the nature of provision made, and those responsible for provision

Removing Barriers to Achievement
Government's Strategy for SEN

- **Early intervention** for children with SEN and access to suitable childcare for parents
- **Removing barriers to learning** access improved by embedding inclusive practice
- **Raising expectations and achievement** (through all national strategies, Sure Start) – personalised learning, assessment for learning, staff CPD
- **Delivering improvements in partnership** to ensure parent confidence

STATUTORY FRAMEWORK FOR MONITORING AND EVALUATION OF SEN POLICY AND PROVISION IN SCHOOLS AND MAINTAINED NURSERIES

- Disability Discrimination Act 1995
- SEN and Disability Act (SENDA) 2001
- SEN Code of Practice 2001
- Government Strategy for SEN, RBA four key areas
- *Every Child Matters* Five outcomes for children
- OFSTED integrated inspection framework for Children's Services
- National Service Framework for Children, Young People and Maternity Services – 11 quality standards for health, social care and some education services

Every Child Matters
Five outcome measures for children

- Being healthy
- Staying safe
- Enjoying and achieving
- Making a positive contribution
- Achieving (social) and economic wellbeing

LA STATUTORY DUTIES FOR SEN
SEN Code of Practice and SENDA

- identify and assess needs of SEN children, matching with additional appropriate provision;
- provide high quality support and service delivery to schools, disseminating good practice;
- improve accessibility to curriculum, premises and written information for pupils with SEN and disability;
- develop co-ordinated multi-agency SEN provision;
- provide independent consultation service for parents/carers of SEN children and young people;
- plan strategically with schools and other significant partners to develop systems for monitoring and accountability for SEN;
- keep under review LA arrangements for SEN provision (quality assurance check, value added);
- promote high standards in education for SEN pupils – reviewing attainment, progress of SEN pupils.

SCHOOL STATUTORY DUTIES FOR SEN
SEN Code of Practice and SENDA

- secure SEN provision for any pupil identified as having SEN;
- ensure that the pupils' SEN are known to all those likely to teach and support them;
- ensure that teachers in school are aware of the importance of identifying and providing for SEN pupils;
- ensure the pupil with SEN engages in activities of the school, together with children who don't have SEN;
- inform parents/carers of a decision made by the school that their child has SEN;
- plan, over time, to increase access to the curriculum, to premises, and to written information;
- take reasonable steps to ensure disabled pupils or prospective pupils aren't placed at a substantial disadvantage, either in relation to admission arrangements to the school, or associated services provided by, or on behalf of, the school.

Table 1.2 The government's Programme of Change

Removing Barriers to Achievement: Government's Strategy for SEN

Four key areas:
- **Early intervention**
- **Removing barriers to learning**
- **Raising expectations and achievement**
- **Delivering improvements in partnership**

Every Child Matters

Five outcomes for children: being healthy, staying safe, enjoying and achieving, making a positive contribution, achieving economic wellbeing

Early intervention and effective protection

Improving information sharing between agencies (common databases and indexes)

Developing a common assessment framework across services – covering SEN, Connexions, Youth Offending Teams, Health & Social Services

Introducing a named 'Lead Professional' to co-ordinate services for children to meet their needs

Developing 'wraparound' care multi-disciplinary service delivery in and around schools and in Children's Centres

Safeguarding Children partnership arrangements

Common occupational standards for all agencies working with children (Workforce Reform)

Integrated inspection framework for Children's Services

NATIONAL SERVICE FRAMEWORK FOR CHILDREN, YOUNG PEOPLE AND MATERNITY SERVICES

Eleven quality standards for health, social care and some education services. Implementation over next ten years and for children and young people under 19.

Part 1 Five core universal standards for all in:
Promoting Health and Wellbeing – Identifying Needs and Intervening Early; Supporting Parenting; Child, Young Person and Family Centred Services; Growing up into Adulthood; Safeguarding and Promoting the Welfare of Children and Young People.

Part 2 Five standards covering services for children, young people needing more specialised care, treatment or support:
Children and Young People who are Ill; Services for Children and Young People in Hospital; Disabled Children and Young People and those with Complex Health Needs; The Mental Health and Psychological well-being of Children and Young People; Medicines for Children and Young People.

Part 3 One standard for pregnant women and their partners: Maternity Services.

THE FIVE-YEAR STRATEGY FOR CHILDREN AND LEARNERS

Children's Centres – in schools or on school sites; one-stop shops 8am–6pm providing range of services, outreach

Extended Full Service Schools

Every school a Healthy School

Widening of Primary Curriculum – PE/sport, play music, learn a language

Networks of Primary Schools supporting and challenging each other

Building Schools for the Future – refurbished, rebuilt secondary schools

Specialist schools expanding, with some to have second specialism, e.g. SEN, and more **Academies**

Foundation partnerships – schools having collective responsibilities for aspects, e.g. SEN, 14–19 curriculum, school improvement, excluded pupils

KS3 Strategy to Secondary Strategy for pupils aged 11–16 from April 2005

New Relationship with Schools – school self-evaluation, data analysis, school improvement partner

New School Profile – information to parents about services offered

Three-Year Budgets for schools

CHILDREN ACT 2004

Children's Commissioner appointed to represent children's views and interests, and report on progress

Local Safeguarding Boards established in LAs

Children's Trusts established securing integrated service delivery in community, localities

Children and Young People's Plan in all LAs

Director of Children's Services in all LAs

Lead Council Member for Children's Services

Promotion of the achievement of Looked After Children

Joint Area Reviews of Children's Services through use of integrated inspection framework

Improved information sharing systems for children and families to speed up the process of obtaining the help and support they need

---

TEN-YEAR STRATEGY FOR CHILDCARE

Covers children from birth to 14 years. Aims to develop flexible, accessible, affordable high quality childcare services to meet needs of children, young people and families.
Provides increased choice to parents to help improve work-life balance.

Sure Start Children's Centre's in every community by 2010

15 hours per week for 38 weeks free educare for children aged 3–4 by 2010

Expanding maternity leave entitlement to nine months paid maternity leave from 2007

Increase in Childcare element of working Tax Credit – from April 2005 (£175 for one child and £300 for two or more children)

Childcare for 5–14 year olds based in schools, with affordable school-based childcare on weekdays for 5–11 year olds between 8 a.m. and 6 p.m.

Secondary schools open on weekdays by 2010 from 8 a.m. to 6 p.m. all year round offering a range of activities such as music, arts, sport, ICT

Transformation Fund of £125 million from April 2005 to support LA childcare investment

All full-time day care settings led by graduate qualified early years professionals

Improved qualifications and status of early years childcare workers

Introduction of a new legal framework for the regulation and inspection of early education and childcare services

Greater partnership working between LAs, childcare providers and Children's Trusts

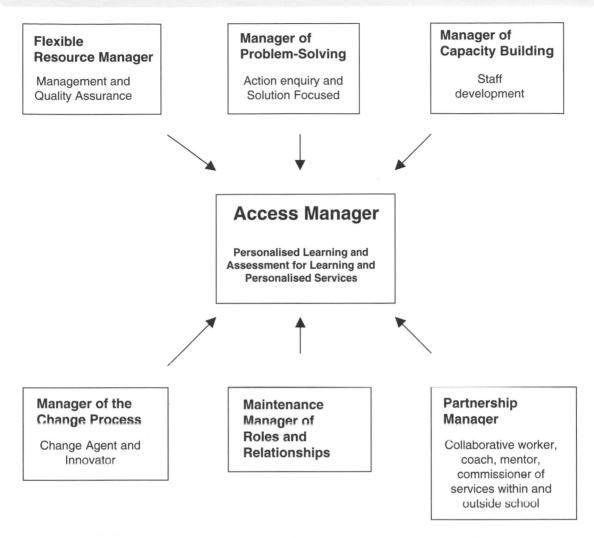

Figure 1.1 SENCOs' strategic management role

educational needs) and their parents/carers are a priority group in the government's educational agenda for raising standards and improving wellbeing.

The Organisation for Economic Co-operation and Development (OECD) (2003) acknowledged the work of UK SENCOs in relation to developing a strategic approach to inclusion:

> In the best inclusive practice SENCOs are fully integrated into the school as a whole, both sharing in the teaching and being members of the school's management team as problem solvers, not just in relation to SEN, but in regard to problems generally. They also have some expertise in aspects of school life affecting all children, for example, in assessment of pupils' progress or in staff appraisal. Where these SENCO roles are developed fully, their posts were highly regarded, much sought after, and recognised as stepping stones to school leadership positions.

The Chief HMI in his Annual Report 2003/2004 noted two key factors in relation to the SENCO role and inclusion:

> The most effective SENCOs in primary and secondary schools are influential in training staff and use their time and expertise very efficiently to support pupils and staff. They also have a high profile and a well-established leadership and management role. Effective inclusion is very closely associated with strong leadership and management and an underpinning commitment to translate policy into practice. (OFSTED 2005b)

Leading-edge opportunities for SENCOs centre on the development of extended full-service schools, networks, personalised learning and personalised services.

Extended schools

Extended schools are at the heart of the change process because they provide opportunities and services for pupils, families and the communities beyond the traditional school timetable. Services can include childcare, lifelong learning, healthcare and social services, cultural and sporting activities and some key public services such as post offices or social clubs. Many schools already offer aspects of extended services such as breakfast and after-school clubs, which improve children's motivation and engagement with learning. Extended schools have great potential to transform lives by providing learning activities and cultural experiences for all, and can offer easily accessible help and support that reflects and responds to the needs of the local community.

All schools, over time, will provide a core of extended services either on site or across a cluster of local schools and providers. For primary schools this includes study support, family learning and parental support opportunities, and better referral systems to multi-agency support where needed. For secondary schools, the core is similar but may be more extensive, opening up facilities for sports, arts and ICT. SENCOs are already engaging in out-of-hours learning activities with pupils, running parent workshops and becoming involved in family learning activities. As extended schools broaden their range of learning activities and services there will be increased opportunities for SENCOs and members of Learning Change Teams in schools (TAs and HLTAs) to apportion and utilise their time more flexibly within the extended school day (8 a.m. to 6 p.m.), i.e. split-shift working (8 a.m.–1 p.m.; 1 p.m.–6 p.m). Some SENCOs may wish to adopt the all-embracing strategic role of Extended School Manager.

Networks

Transformation involves schools getting together in networks to innovate, led by 'champions' of good practice, e.g. Leading SENCOs, ASTs for SEN, Excellent Teachers for SEN, working alongside SEN and inclusion advisers and consultants from LAs or private companies.

Networks are mechanisms where participants collaborate for mutual benefit and exchange skills, best practice, expertise and resources in order to solve problems and seek solutions. They feed the creative co-production of new knowledge that helps to support smarter professional practice for new ways of working in teams, and to renew the professional pride of SENCOs.

Combining innovation with networks is the key to successful innovation and empowering SENCOs. Innovation is about exploiting a new idea which, through practical action, adds value to a process, service or product. SENCOs cannot afford not to innovate.

Networks are based on the premise of a fundamental cultural shift in the way schools operate and function. The move is towards a new order of school that is networked and collaborative, with leadership distributed within and between schools and other agencies. For example, SENCOs in their networks may wish to focus on developing the pupils' 'voice', or on improving KS2 to KS3 transition for pupils with more complex SEN in mainstream, e.g. ASD, by utilising the best practice exemplar material in the National Service Framework Standard 8 for disabled children, young people and those with complex health needs, as a benchmark for multi-agency partnership working. Networks can be 'virtual', with SENCOs coaching partners and sharing best practice via e-learning systems: telephone conferencing and text messaging, e-mail-conferencing, using electronic SENCO forums on school websites and the Becta NGfL inclusion website.

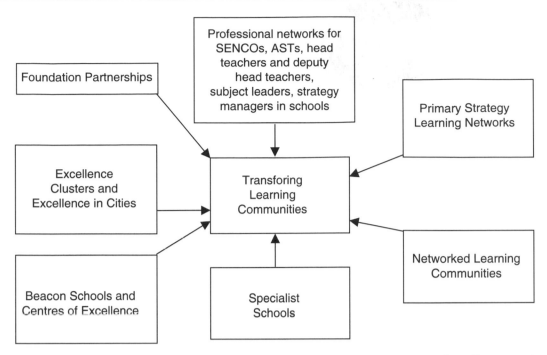

Figure 1.2 Map of networks transforming learning communities (Farrar and Walker 2005)

Networks linked in with extended schools or foundation partnerships may see the 'virtual' SENCO communicating with and working across a number of schools within a federation or cluster of schools, e.g. in networks comprising small rural schools. Learning networks provide a wide range of learning experiences, enabled by powerful ICT and open learning resources. Community interests are expressed in the form of learning for different cultures and values.

Advantages of networks to SENCOs

Networks help to:

- foster innovation, risk taking and 'thinking outside the box';
- act as a test bed for new ideas;
- provide challenge and discipline to professionals and practitioners in schools and services;
- integrate services and act as a gateway to shared resources;
- build effective relationships between staff, pupils, parents, services and the community;
- promote greater openness and sharing of best practice and expertise;
- raise expectations of all stakeholders;
- share vision, objectives, ownership, leadership and management and professional development;
- promote co-working between partner schools;
- involve and inform pupils, parents, governors, LA children's services; and
- foster good, open, two-way communication.

Effective networks:

- design around a compelling idea, aspirational purpose or agreed collective priority;
- focus on pupil learning;
- create new opportunities for adult learning; and
- have dedicated leadership and management.

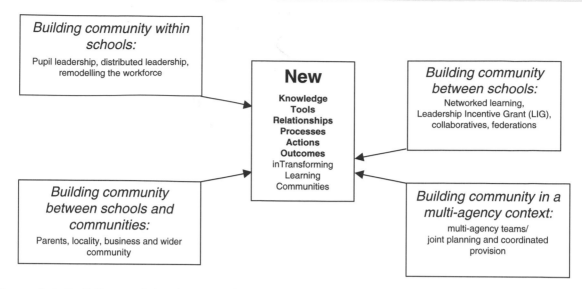

Figure 1.3 Building and developing school and community networks and strategic partnerships (Farrar and Walker 2005)

New relationships across schools and sectors are underpinned and driven by five key factors:

- greater focus on the child and family through *Every Child Matters: Change for Children*;
- re-conceptualisation of professions – remodelling the workforce;
- a commitment to personalisation in all major government strategies;
- a commitment to stakeholder empowerment (Five Year Strategy); and
- greater understanding of interdependency of home, school and community, e.g. National Standards for Headteachers – Standard 6 *Strengthening Community*, which would be just as relevant to SENCOs.

The change process that SENCOs will need to go through in removing barriers to achievement and in meeting the five outcomes for children and young people in *Every Child Matters: Change for Children in Schools* is outlined below.

Schools will be challenged to align, accumulate and transfer their SEN and inclusion knowledge more effectively in order to achieve sustainable progress, not just within schools, but also in the wider learning community and network. In any process of change there are four stages in transformation:

- creating the right climate for risk taking, experimentation and removing any 'blame culture' if an idea does not work;

Table 1.3 The change process for SENCOs

Understand and appreciate	Discover	Deepen	Develop and experience	Deliver
Starting to address issues	This is bigger than first thought	It is tough but a solution can be found	There is a strategy and a plan for future success	Some issues have been resolved and a way forward has been found
Mutual respect	Commitment	Clarity	Openness	Trust

- disciplined innovation – avoiding innovation overload by focusing on one or two priorities that can be well managed within a school and across a networked community, working in partnership; high impact for small energy input (SMART working);
- going lateral – spreading new practice on a peer-to-peer basis (coaching and mentoring) through networks, where an initiative or idea is adopted because it will be of real benefit to pupils, and make working more effective and better for stakeholders; best practice has to be demonstrated in new contexts within a network (co-creativity);
- ICT to complement face-to-face SENCO partnership working through electronic communication systems and multimedia CPD training programmes.

Personalised learning

This involves decisive progress in educational standards where every child matters. It encourages a focus on the totality of resources available for learning at home and in school. Pupils are participants in personalisation and are encouraged from an early age and from all social backgrounds to become more involved in making decisions about what they would like to learn and how. As more active learners, pupils would also have more of a part in setting targets for themselves and in devising their own learning plans.

The purpose of personalised learning is to promote personal development through self-realisation, self-enhancement and self-development. The child and young person is viewed as an active, responsible and self-motivated learner. Personalised learning encourages learning to take place in holidays and outside school hours.

Personalised learning will only be successful if pupils are engaged in continual, self-critical assessment of their talents, achievements, performance, learning strategies and targets, so that they can adjust their learning approaches. This assessment for learning means that children and young people can set the pace and purpose of their learning. In a personalised system, a central function of assessment is to help pupils understand what they have been learning and doing, and how they can improve.

Five key components of personalised learning:

- **Assessment for learning**: where the strengths and weaknesses of individual children and young people are known by all those who work with them. Tracking pupil progress and setting individual learning and/or behaviour targets can help to tackle underperformance through the collection and analysis of performance data. These pupil performance data also provide structured feedback to pupils and help teachers to plan lessons according to personalised learning needs.
- **Effective teaching and learning strategies**: improve the management of pupils' learning experiences by providing a range of learning opportunities within and beyond school hours through:
  - (a) utilising a range of learning approaches, e.g. whole-class; group and paired work; individual learning;
  - (b) using ICT and multimedia technology to enhance and extend learning;
  - (c) giving pupils greater ownership and control over their own learning.
- **Curriculum entitlement and choice**: provides flexible learning pathways, opportunities for enrichment and creativity and opportunities to learn across educational settings.
- **School organisation:** workforce remodelling meets the demands of personalised learning by providing planning, preparation and assessment (PPA) time for teachers; 'virtual' schools

provide on-line learning materials and support for learning for children, young people and families. Teachers become facilitators of learning, rather than front-line deliverers of learning.

- **Strong partnership beyond the school**: parents/carers are involved more proactively in their child's learning, behaviour management and attendance at school. Regular parent workshops in school enable parents to work together with teachers and their children and this helps to increase participation and interest levels. SENCOs can play a lead role in organising and running these workshops. Children who are excluded from school, or who are vulnerable and 'at risk', require a personal advocate who may come from within or outside the school (and who may be the SENCO) to help them in assembling the solutions needed from a range of personalised services.

How SENCOs can prepare for a personalisation role:

- collaborate on specific initiatives or aspects of personalised learning and personalised services in networks, foundation partnerships and clusters (co-creativity; co-working);
- draw on facilities and resources in the network and wider community (commissioning);
- build on and contribute to community cohesion by adopting a multi-agency focus to meet SEN pupils' holistic needs (solution-assembler; networker);
- strengthen links between home, school and services by keeping in regular contact and communicating in preferred medium, e.g. electronically or face-to-face (advocate);
- realise that the school is not the only place where learning takes place; therefore engage with other places and means of learning for pupils (change champion);
- take an active part in utilising ICT and multimedia technology to support own role and CPD, as well as that of pupils and their parents/carers (facilitator of learning);
- become an ambassador for promoting SEN and inclusion provision within the community and network;
- listen to and respond to the needs of SEN pupils and their parents (consumer demand) by providing the necessary information and services (knowledge manger; solution assembler); and
- seek sponsorship from local business and community partners (innovator).

Further activities for SENCOs

The questions below on each aspect covered in this chapter will enable SENCOs to discuss and resolve issues within their own school and also across networks and clusters.

Extended schools

- How can SENCOs enable SEN pupils and their parents/carers to play a role in shaping the services offered by a school, by giving them a 'voice'?
- What are the greatest practical barriers to involving parents and other community members in the school's SEN and inclusion activities and developments? How can these barriers be overcome?
- Is it about bringing more people into the school, or is it more about taking the school out to the community?
- How will the SENCO enable parents/carers of pupils with SEN and disability to be co-producers of extended school services?

Networks and cross-service working

- Can you identify any risks and/or dangers in networking? If so, what are they and how can these be overcome?
- What action might you take as SENCO to create the right climate for innovation in your school?
- What do you need to do in your school to ensure the transfer of good practice from SENCO networks?
- Which aspects of your current team working and strategic leadership role for SEN equip your school in becoming more effective in cross-sector working?
- What important change would you make in relation to the SENCO role in order to enhance greater cross-sector working?
- What is the extent of your current cross-sector working practice as SENCO?
- As a SENCO, what new relationships do you want to transform or build in to current networks?

Personalisation

- How can your pupils with SEN and disabilities have the capacity or opportunity to make informed choices about what and how they learn?
- How can pupils with SEN and disability be enabled to further develop their capacity in decision-making about their learning and SEN provision?
- Can SEN pupils be involved in all decisions, or are there some issues that should be resolved without their involvement? If so, what are they?
- How can pupils become more involved in their own assessment for learning? What works and what does not work for particular groups of pupils?
- How can the SENCO recognise the different kinds of learning that go beyond the classroom for pupils with SEN?
- What is the role of the SENCO in a personalised education system?
- How can non-teaching staff be used to facilitate more personalised learning?
- How might the school organisation need to change in a personalised system?
- Who else (agencies, organisations or professionals) should be involved to ensure that the needs of the 'whole' learner are met?
- In the new future personalisation process, as SENCO, what will you do to effect change in your school:
    - over the next term?
    - by the end of the academic year?
    - in two years' time?

2

Every Child Matters and the Evolving SENCO Role

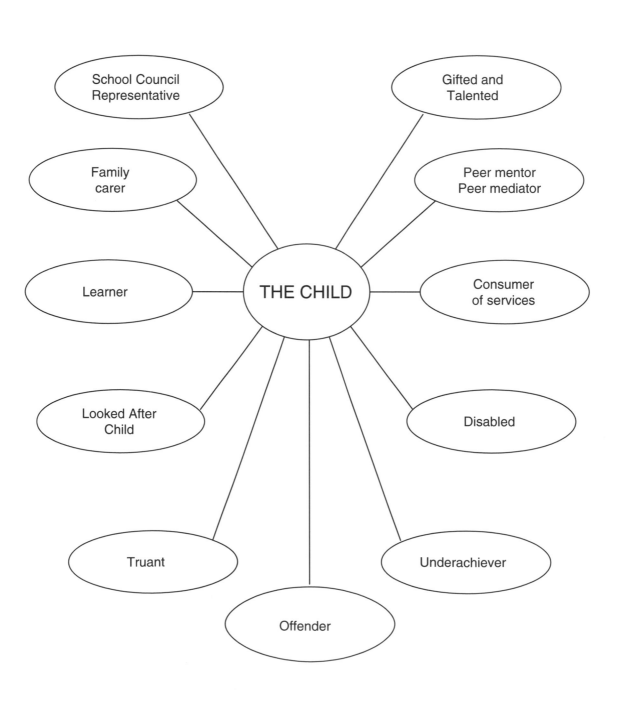

Schools as service providers to children and families

The philosophy behind the government's Change for Children programme is to protect, nurture and improve the life chances of children and young people, in particular those of vulnerable children.

> Raising standards in schools and inclusion go hand in hand. In particular, schools have a critical role in raising the educational achievement of children in care, and other groups that have consistently underachieved. (DfES 2004f: 4.6)

Undoubtedly, *Every Child Matters* considerably increases the responsibility and accountability of SENCOs working in extended schools, because it is such a wide, complex, ambitious and far-reaching educational agenda.

The tables on the following pages summarise the development of *Every Child Matters* from consultation stage to legislation. Everyone working in a school has a role to play in a local programme of change for children, whether they are a head teacher, teacher, teaching assistant, site manager, governor, or pupil.

Schools already contribute to pupils' wider wellbeing by:

- helping each pupil achieve the highest educational standards they possibly can;
- dealing with bullying and discrimination, and keeping children safe;
- becoming Healthy Schools and promoting healthy lifestyles through Personal, Social and Health Education (PSHE) lessons, drugs education, breakfast clubs and sporting activities;
- ensuring attendance, encouraging pupils to behave responsibly, giving them a strong 'voice' in the life of the school and encouraging them to help others in school and in the community;
- helping communities to value education and be aware that it is the route out of the poverty trap; and
- engaging and helping parents in actively supporting their children's learning and development.

Schools acting as 'hubs' for lifelong learning and personalised services for children, young people and families have an opportunity to extend their provision to meet the needs of their local community, and to get to know their client/consumer groups better. Lisa, aged 16–18, commented:

> I like the idea of schools being more open and being used by the wider community. I think the youth and the rest of the community are separated and need to be more involved and know about what is going on. This applies to the community knowing about what the school is doing and the schools knowing about what is going on in the community. (DfES 2004f: 8)

Schools providing services needed by local people become the focus of the local community and boost community pride and involvement.

Role of social care professionals working in schools

The role of social workers and social care workers is:

- to safeguard and promote the welfare of children and young people;
- to engage in multi-agency partnership working with other services;
- to contribute to the common assessment process for children, analyse information in order to make judgements about risks to a child's welfare, and how to promote the educational achievement of a child in public care; and

Table 2.1 The Green Paper

Key areas	Outline of proposals
Introduction	Consultation document issued in September 2003. Provided an outline of how the government wants to address the needs of children at risk in the context of improving services for all children and young people. Based on five outcomes and priorities for children and young people: being healthy, staying safe, enjoying and achieving, making a positive contribution, economic wellbeing. Put forward ideas and proposals for reforming the delivery of a range of services for children, young people and their families.
1. Supporting parents and carers	■ Universal services (health, social services, childcare) providing information and advice, and engaging parents in supporting their child's development. ■ Targeted and specialist support available to parents of children and young people requiring additional support (SEN, disability). ■ Compulsory action through Parenting Orders for those parents condoning their child's truancy, antisocial behaviour, offending. ■ Promotion of foster care.
2. Early intervention and effective protection	■ Improving information sharing between agencies so each is clear about the services children have had contact with. ■ Developing a common assessment framework across services for children, covering SEN, Connexions, Youth Offending Teams, health and social services. ■ Introducing a 'lead professional' to be responsible for ensuring a coherent package of services to meet the child's needs. This professional can be from within a school, or from an external agency. ■ Developing 'on-the-spot' service delivery from professionals working in multi-disciplinary teams based in and around schools and Children's Centres, who will provide rapid response to concerns of teachers, childcare workers and others.
3. Accountability and integration	■ Director of Children's Services in all Local Authorities (LAs). ■ Lead elected council member for children in all LAs. ■ Children's Trusts created which will bring together a range of services and report to elected members in the LA. ■ Local Safeguarding Children's Board created in all LAs. ■ New Government Minister for Children, Young People and Families. ■ A Children's Commissioner to be appointed, as independent champion for children, reporting annually to Parliament.
4. Workforce reform	■ Strategy to improve skills and effectiveness of the children's workforce. ■ High-profile recruitment campaign. ■ Workload survey to reduce bureaucracy to enable more direct work with children and families. ■ Flexible training routes in social work. ■ Common occupational standards across children's practice, linked to modular qualifications. ■ Common core training for those working with children and families. ■ Leadership development programme. ■ DfES Children's Workforce Unit created which develops a pay and workforce strategy. ■ Establishment of Sector Skills Council (SSC) for Children and Young People's Services to deliver key parts of the Workforce Reform Strategy.

Model *Every Child Matters* SEN Policy Statement

Every pupil with SEN and disability in this inclusive school has an entitlement to fulfil his/her optimum potential. This is achieved by ensuring the wellbeing of all pupils in relation to: being healthy, staying safe, enjoying and achieving, making a positive contribution, and achieving social and economic wellbeing.

These wellbeing outcomes are embraced in every aspect of school life: personalised teaching and learning approaches; access to ICT across the curriculum; flexible learning pathways and out-of-hours learning activities; support for emotional wellbeing; flexible timetables; assessment for learning which engages pupils in having a say about their progress and SEN provision; and partnership with parents/carers, other schools, the local community and with personalised 'wraparound' health care and social service providers.

Table 2.2 Next Steps

Key areas	Summary of Next Steps
1. Introduction and feedback from initial consultation	Next Steps was published in March 2004, to coincide with the Children Bill. The document describes the government's response following consultation, and the next steps towards developing a shared programme of change for children, as well as the work already in progress to strengthen partnership working in order to achieve the five outcomes for children.
2. The Children Bill	The Children Bill provided the first legislative step for developing more effective and accessible services focused around the needs of children, young people and their families, in their local area. The Bill created: ■ clear, shared outcomes across services embedded in legislation; ■ an independent champion for the views and interests of children who will report on how these outcomes are changing; ■ robust partnership arrangements to ensure that public, private, voluntary and community sector organisations work together to improve these outcomes; ■ a tighter focus on local arrangements for child protection; ■ clearer accountability for children's services; ■ a new integrated inspection framework to ensure that services are judged on how they effectively work together to achieve better outcomes and to promote continuous improvement, with intervention powers in areas falling below minimum standards; ■ a legislative basis for better sharing of information, and other detailed measures to improve services; ■ Local Safeguarding Children Boards in every LA to co-ordinate and ensure the effectiveness of local arrangements and services to safeguard children; ■ commissioning of children's services with a wide range of partners – developing Children's Trusts in all LAs by 2008, to ensure integrated service delivery, and effective use of pooled budgets and resources.
3. Towards a shared programme of change	■ **Maximising opportunities and minimising risks** – helping children to fulfil their potential and supporting families throughout a child's and young person's life. ■ **Early intervention** – government's SEN Strategy aiming for an inclusive system, whereby children with SEN can have their needs met in school, without having to have a statement. Early identification of disabilities and better response from services supporting families. National Service Framework for Children, Young People and Maternity Services setting evidence-based standards for health, social care services covering the interface of these services with education. Youth justice proposals for educational engagement, mentoring and better parenting. ■ **Whole system change** – sharper accountability, more robust partnerships, targets and performance management; greater consistency in Standards across services; simpler and more flexible resource management with decisions taken at front-line; greater skill investment in those working with children, young people and families; support for improvement and culture change – scooping the market for children's services, removing political, economic and cultural barriers to commissioning and provision of information to client groups; simplifying contractual arrangements. ■ **Workforce reform** – Sector Skills Council (SSC) to set up a UK Children's Workforce Network of all those working with children, young people and families, including those working in health, law enforcement, sport, recreation, and schools; establishment of Children, Young People and Families Council. TTA responsible for occupational standards and training for all staff from services working with children, young people. DfES/Cabinet Office Regulatory Impact Unit – identifying causes of unnecessary bureaucracy and recommending a practical set of actions.
4. Working in partnership	■ Co-operation in working, across services, i.e. health services, schools, Learning Skills Council (LSC), Connexions, police, probation service, Family Justice system, voluntary and community sectors. ■ Removing barriers to participation in service planning and service delivery. ■ Personalisation in learning, care and support. ■ Closer working between schools, Children's Trusts, communities and specialist services.

Table 2.3 Change for Children

Key areas	Summary of Change for Children
Introduction	Change for Children was issued in December 2004. Four accompanying documents related specifically to: schools, social care, criminal justice system, and health services. It explained the national framework for local change programmes in order to build services around the needs of children and young people. It set out the action needed at local level in order to: <ul><li>improve and integrate universal services in early years settings, schools and the health service;</li><li>provide more specialised help to act early and effectively to prevent and address problems;</li><li>reconfigure services around the child and family in one place, e.g. Children's Centre, extended schools, multi-disciplinary teams of professionals;</li><li>ensure dedicated and enterprising leadership at all levels of the system;</li><li>develop a shared sense of responsibility across agencies for safeguarding and protecting children from harm;</li><li>listen to children and young people and their families when assessing and planning service provision, and in direct delivery.</li></ul>
1. National framework for local change programmes	**The Children Act** (15 November 2004) established: <ul><li>a Children's Commissioner to champion the views and interests of children and young people;</li><li>a duty on LAs to make arrangements to promote co-operation between agencies and other appropriate bodies (such as voluntary and community organisations) in order to improve children's wellbeing in relation to the five outcomes for children in *Every Child Matters*, and a duty on key partners to participate in the co-operation arrangements;</li><li>a duty on key agencies to safeguard and promote the welfare of children;</li><li>a duty on LAs to set up Local Safeguarding Children Boards and on key partners to take part;</li><li>provision for indexes or databases containing basic information about children and young people to enable better sharing of information;</li><li>a requirement for a single Children and Young People's Plan to be drawn up by each Local Authority;</li><li>a requirement on LAs to appoint a Director of Children's Services and designate a Lead Member;</li><li>the creation of an integrated inspection framework and the conduct of Joint Area Reviews to assess local areas' progress in improving outcomes; and</li><li>provisions relating to foster care, private fostering and the education of children in care.</li></ul> The National Service Framework for Children, Young People and Maternity Services (NSF) is integral to the implementation of the Children Act 2004, and local change programmes. Local change programmes will be stronger if set within a supportive national framework comprising key elements: policies and products, improvement cycle, supporting change, inspection criteria, targets and indicators, outcomes and aims.
2. Working towards better outcomes for children and young people	Five outcomes for children are central to the change programme; they are interdependent, and show important relationships between educational achievement and wellbeing. **The Outcomes Framework** will enable LAs with their partners to carry out a thorough needs analysis as a starting point for planning a local change programme. The results of the needs analysis will allow LAs and their partners to establish and agree their vision to improve outcomes for children and young people, to set priorities for action and to agree local targets. The Outcomes Framework will enable local children's services to be held accountable for delivering improved outcomes through integrated inspections using common criteria, developed with reference to the National Service Framework (NSF).
3. Integrated services and local change	Securing a shift from intervention to prevention, and meeting the needs of the most vulnerable. This re-shaping requires personalised and high quality, integrated universal services, which give easy access to effective and targeted specialist services, which will be delivered by a skilled and effective workforce, and utilise joint commissioning and pooled budgets.
4. Support for local change	Regional Change Advisers based in Government Offices supporting local areas in planning and implementing the local change programme; training for elected members in LAs; disseminating good practice on Children's Trusts; performance review, monitoring and assessment through integrated inspection of children's services; additional funding to LAs to support the Change for Children programme.

Table 2.4 Five possible outcomes

Outcome	ECM descriptor	OFSTED descriptor
Being healthy	Physically, mentally and emotionally healthy; sexually healthy; healthy lifestyles; choose not to take illegal drugs; parents/carers/families promote healthy choices	Take regular exercise, including at least two hours PE and sport a week; know about and make healthy lifestyle choices; understand sexual health risks and the dangers of smoking and substance abuse; eat and drink healthily; recognise the signs of personal stress and develop strategies to manage it
Staying safe	Safe from maltreatment, neglect, violence, sexual exploitation; safe from accidental injury and death; safe from bullying and discrimination; safe from crime and anti-social behaviour in and out of school; have security, stability and are cared for; parents/carers/families provide safe homes and stability	Display concern for others and refrain from intimidating and anti-social behaviour; feel safe from bullying and discrimination; feel confident to report bullying and racist incidents; act responsibly in high-risk situations
Enjoying and achieving	Ready for school; attend and enjoy school; achieve stretching national educational standards in primary and secondary school; achieve personal and social development and enjoy recreation; parents/carers/families support learning	Have positive attitudes to education, behave well and have a good school attendance record
Making a positive contribution	Engage in decision-making and support the community and environment; engage in law-abiding and positive behaviour in and out of school; develop positive relationships and choose not to bully and discriminate; develop self-confidence and successfully deal with significant life changes and challenges; develop enterprising behaviour; parents/carers/families promote positive behaviour	Understand their legal and civil rights and responsibilities; show social responsibility, and refrain from bullying and discrimination; express their views at school and are confident their views and 'voice' will be heard; initiate and manage a range of organised activities in school and community organisations
Achieving economic and social wellbeing	Engage in further education, employment or training on leaving school; ready for employment; live in decent homes and sustainable communities; access to transport and material goods; live in households free from low income; parents/carers/families are supported to be economically active	Develop basic skills in literacy, numeracy and ICT; develop their self-confidence and team working skills; become enterprising, able to handle change, take initiative, and calculate risk when making decisions; become financially literate and gain an understanding of business and the economy and of their career options; develop knowledge and skills when they are older, related to workplace situations

For a more detailed Outcomes Framework see
http://www.everychildmatters.gov.uk/_files/8FDC0C06EA8CD5A77CCDA888EED28FDF.pdf

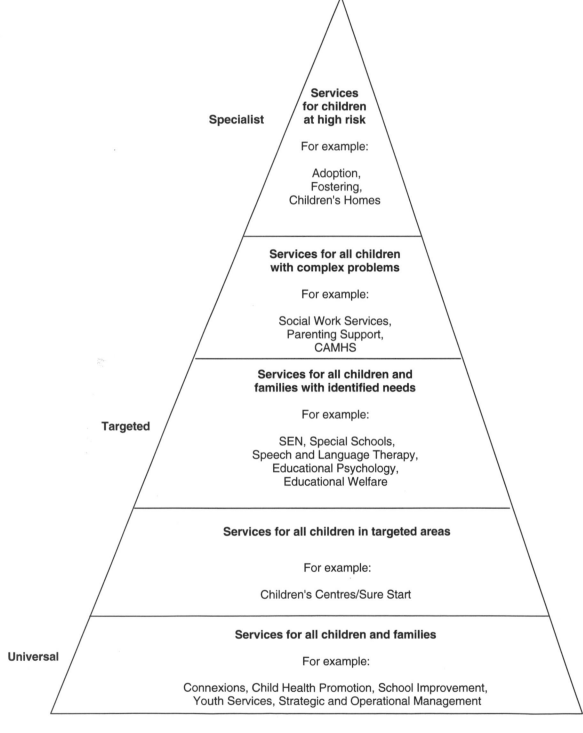

Figure 2.1 Universal, targeted and specialist services in and around schools

Table 2.5 Implications of *Every Child Matters* for the SENCO role (adapted from DfES 2003a)

Every Child Matters aspect	New role for SENCO
Early intervention and effective protection	**Lead Professional** – where SENCO has daily contact with child in school; promotes welfare of child and safeguarding children; ensures children with additional needs receive co-ordinated support from different agencies; effective 'gatekeeper' for information sharing to support service delivery; identifies holistic needs of children who are not achieving the five outcomes of *Every Child Matters* (ECM) with other professionals from Health, Social Services, Education.
Supporting parents and carers	**Advocate, Knowledge/Information Manager** – SENCO mediates individual pupils' relationships with services required; contributes to the School Profile, which sets out for parents the full range of services offered at the school for children and young people and their families; enables and empowers parents/carers – gathering their views and using these to inform service provision; maintains home–school liaison; explains the Common Assessment process to parents/carers.
Scoping children's services	**Commissioner and Broker** – SENCO with head teacher will be involved in researching service provider options in the local market and exploring models of service delivery; involved in liaison and co-ordination with providers, via the Children's Trust; brokering and commissioning support from various sources: e.g. LA, mainstream schools, special schools, clusters, networks, and from voluntary and community organisations; SENCO determining and forecasting needs of children; contracting and procuring services, and arranging and reviewing contracts from service providers with the head teacher.
Pooled budgets between services	**Resource Manager** – SENCO with the head teacher and school bursar will know the SEN budget for the year, and be a budget holder; SENCO will provision map for SEN and mobilise a range of resources from within and outside the school, which are cost-effective and respond to the needs of children, and families in the community; SENCO operates Best Value principles: challenge, compare, consult and compete when making spending decisions.
Multi-disciplinary teams of para-professionals	**Partnership Manager** – SENCO is critically engaged in multi-agency working; mobilising and deploying professionals from multi-agency services within school in effective and efficient ways to improve targeted pupils' learning, behaviour, personal and social development and wellbeing. SENCO responsible for integrating para-professional team successfully into school organisation, ensuring they are familiar with school culture, policy, practice and administrative systems. SENCO uses Common Assessment information to develop individual action plans for targeted children and parents; SENCO clarifies and agrees targets and goals with para-professionals from external agencies.
Integrated inspections of children's services	**Quality Assurance** – SENCO monitoring and evaluating SEN policy, provision and extended services against OFSTED criteria (ECM five outcomes) and the National Standards Framework (NSF) Standards, through annual school self-evaluation process; tracking pupil progress and analysing data to identify rates of pupil progress, attainment, achievement and wellbeing in relation to impact of additional interventions and provision put in place; SENCO will also contribute to monitoring SEN pupils following flexible learning pathways at 14–19.
Personalisation in learning, care and support	**Facilitator** – of personalised learning and 'wraparound care' services for SEN pupils; advising teachers and TAs on curriculum access, teaching and learning approaches, appropriate learning pathways; behaviour management; providing opportunities for personal development for SEN pupils; clarifying roles of para-professionals supporting SEN pupils in the school/classroom with teachers/TAs; clarifying SENCO, teachers/TA's role with para-professionals from services.

(Continued)

Table 2.5 (*Continued*)

Every Child Matters aspect	New role for SENCO
Needs analysis using *Every Child Matters* outcomes framework	**Solution Assembler** – SENCO member of school/multi-professional problem-solving/change team. SENCO with head teacher: ■ feeds views into Children's Trust to inform local service planning as well as school improvement plan priorities; ■ analyses data, which identifies patterns and trends in pupils' needs and outcomes in local area/community; ■ surveys and acts on client/customer views (parents, children) to inform action planning/provision mapping in obtaining appropriate service provision and delivery from providers, aligned to SEN budget; SENCO involved in workforce remodelling for SEN, and in training school staff in relation to SEN/Inclusion.

Table 2.6 Examples of SENCO activities linked to the five outcomes of *Every Child Matters*

Every Child Matters outcome	Example of SENCO activities
Being healthy	SENCO introduces stress management programme for pupils with BESD, which entails aromatherapy, relaxation techniques, in a peaceful multi-sensory room/zone within the school.
Staying safe	SENCO implements peer mediation as a strategy to reduce incidents of bullying and discrimination.
Enjoying and achieving	SENCO ensures pupils with more severe and complex learning difficulties can follow appropriate learning pathways in Key Stage 4, across a range of educational settings and by a range of means, e.g. distance learning, e-learning.
Making a positive contribution	SENCO ensures SEN pupils are involved in school projects and initiatives that engage them in 'real' activities that help others, e.g. Peer mentoring, 'Befriending' scheme
Achieving economic wellbeing	SENCO ensures that SEN pupils are engaged in mini-enterprise projects which help to develop their financial literacy skills, team working skills, build their self-confidence and develop their problem-solving skills.

- to work as part of a multi-disciplinary team in a school-based service hub, or on a 'virtual' basis, working across a cluster or network of schools.

Role of healthcare professionals working with schools:

- increasing the number of school nurses;
- greater integration and co-location of health service practitioners within children's centres, where the health and wellbeing of children can be enhanced;
- nursing, midwifery and health visiting services located as close to a child's home as possible in extended schools, communities, Connexions, Sure Start children's centres, youth justice service;
- supporting Healthy Schools programme – healthy eating in schools, promoting healthy lifestyles, providing confidential health advice, breakfast clubs;
- enabling schools to provide more opportunities for sport and physical activity;
- development of personal health plans for all children;
- contributing directly to *Every Child Matters* outcomes: being healthy, staying safe;

Table 2.7 Example of a School Development Plan implementing *Every Child Matters* outcomes

Priority	ECM outcome number	Activities and actions	Responsibility	Timescale	Resources	Success criteria/ impact on pupils
1. Introduce ECM to inform whole-school policy, planning and culture	1 to 5	(a) Prepare and deliver whole-school INSET on ECM to staff, governors, para-professionals (b) Organise and deliver a drama production involving pupils, based on meeting the outcomes of ECMs, for parents, pupils and community members	SENCO with the head teacher, and other external staff from Health, Social Services and Education English Co-ordinator, SENCO, Head of Performing Arts from FE college	Plan during September for delivery in October January start to prepare and rehearse, for final pro-duction in March	Time to meet and prepare ICT/ multimedia PowerPoint facilities. Printing of handouts Funding scenery and costumes; time to rehearse; printing of programmes and publicity posters	All staff fully understand the implications of ECM and start to link 5 outcomes to their subject policy, development planning and curriculum planning, as well as SDP priority. All stakeholders are clear about inclusion and ECM. Pupils have a strong 'voice'. There is good attendance at performances, from the community.
2. Implement flexible, personalised learning beyond school hours for targeted pupils	3	Working with Subject Leaders/Strategy Manager(s): (a) Produce curriculum materials on CD and on-line for pupils to use at home (b) Provide distance learning facilities – laptop computers (c) Open a cyber-café in Community Centre, adjacent to school site	Co-ordinator for ICT, Deputy head teacher and SENCO ICT Co-ordinator and Head of Community Centre	(a) Planning from October and introduce in January (b) January – July monitor and review (c) January – March and ongoing	Time for staff to meet and plan resources. Cost of CD production. Purchase of additional laptop computers. Sponsorship from local business to equip community centre	Pupils on long-term absence can continue learning out-of-school, at home or abroad, and their attainment improves. Parents proactively support their child's learning outside school. Community has increased access to ICT facilities for lifelong learning and leisure.

(*Continued*)

Table 2.7 (*Continued*)

Priority	ECM outcome number	Activities and actions	Responsibility	Timescale	Resources	Success criteria/ impact on pupils
3. Develop a quiet Peace Zone in School for pupils and staff	1 & 2	(a) Working group of pupils, staff and external business partners set up (b) Business plan produced and Peace Zone established in school	Head teacher, SENCO, and local business sponsor	Working group meet, plan and design (October – February) Zone operational from June, and ongoing	Time for group meetings. Visit to Peace Zone in another school. Cost of refurbishing and fitting out. Peace Zone. Publicity material to launch Peace Zone	Pupils and staff less stressed. Attendance of staff and pupils improves. Peace Zone becomes an example of best practice locally, and has improved considerably the wellbeing of staff and pupils.
4. Introduce mini-enterprise initiatives to engage pupils with SEN and disability	4 & 5	(a) Survey local community needs. (b) Identify target classes to participate. (c) Prepare business plan, design brief, (three projects – one per term with different classes) (d) Make and sell items: bird boxes, cakes, picture frames in local community	Deputy head teacher with DT Co-ordinator, SENCO, and Head of Business Studies from High School	Each term: September to December; January to April; May to July	Time for staff to analyse surveys, identify classes and undertake projects. Purchase of materials at cost (discount from local sponsor). Time for marketing and selling items in School Shop to customers.	Pupils more confident in team working, problem-solving, decision-making and financially literate. Links strengthened with members of local community, e.g. elderly, disabled, parents.

ECM Outcomes: 1 Being healthy; 2 Staying safe; 3 Enjoying and achieving; 4 Making a positive contribution; 5 Achieving economic wellbeing

- consulting with children, young people and families on planning and health service delivery;
- contributing to the assessment of the 'whole child' via common assessment framework;
- contributing to safeguarding and promoting the welfare of children.

Further activities for SENCOs related to *Every Child Matters*

The questions below, on aspects covered in this chapter related to *Every Child Matters*, will enable SENCOs to discuss ways forward in meeting the requirements of their changing role in the context of the government's Change for Children programme:

- What barriers exist in your school currently that are likely to prevent the implementation of *Every Child Matters: Change for Children*?

- What progress has your school already made in starting to address and respond to the five outcomes of *Every Child Matters*?
- What are the next steps necessary in order to embed Every Child Matters strategically in whole-school SEN and Inclusion policy and planning?
- What action do you need to take as a SENCO, in order to ensure the *Every Child Matters: Change for Children* programme is successfully implemented and delivered in school?
- How can the way you manage SEN knowledge become more closely aligned with the five outcomes of *Every Child Matters*?
- Who else will you need to work with, both from within and outside school, in order to implement *Every Child Matters*?
- How do you intend to monitor and evaluate the five outcomes of *Every Child Matters* in your school?
- How do you intend to co-ordinate and monitor those working in a multi-disciplinary para-professional team in your school?
- As a SENCO, what advice would you offer to other SENCOs in a networked learning community of schools about how to implement successfully the *Every Child Matters: Change for Children* programme?

Removing Barriers to Achievement: Implications for the SENCO Role

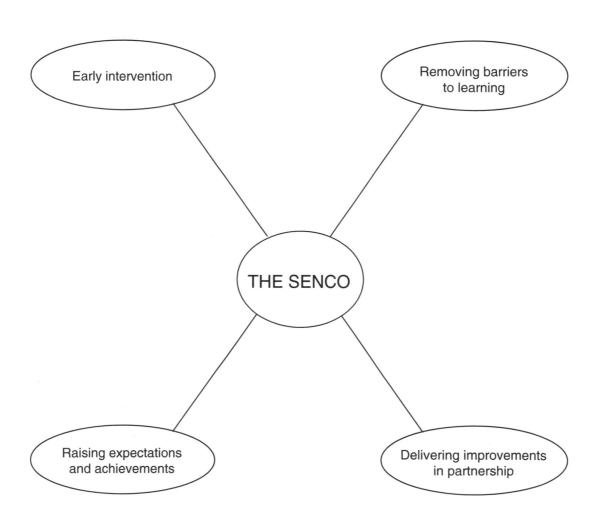

Implications for the SENCO role

The SEN Code of Practice confirmed part of the SENCO role as below:

> The SENCO, with the support of the headteacher and colleagues, seeks to develop effective ways of overcoming barriers to learning and sustaining effective teaching through the analysis and assessment of pupils' needs, by monitoring the quality of teaching and standards of pupils' achievement and by setting targets for improvement. (DfES 2001b: 5.31)

This confirms the SENCO role envisaged in the government's Strategy for SEN, whereby:

> SENCOs play a pivotal role co-ordinating provision across the school and linking class and subject teachers with SEN specialists to improve the quality of teaching and learning. (DfES 2004a 3.14)

Early intervention

Personalised, co-ordinated multi-disciplinary services based around the needs of the child, and their impact on the learning and wellbeing of pupils with SEN, is a key focus to the first chapter of *Removing Barriers to Achievement* (RBA).

Class and subject teachers will have access to SEN specialists working as part of a para-professional team within and across a network of schools, to support and deliver personalised learning. Clearly, the SENCO's co-ordination and management role will be heightened and increased in relation to bringing such a team together in order to intervene early and address the individual needs of pupils with SEN. The SENCO may also work directly with pupils as a member of the para-professional team within school, or in other local schools in a networked learning community, particularly if they have a high level of expertise in an area of SEN, e.g. BESD or ASD.

Head teachers will need to manage the para-SENCO role carefully, in order to ensure that their own good-quality SEN practice is not compromised. I envisage SENCOs being released from the burdens of SEN bureaucracy and having this time taken up with increased liaison and meeting more frequently with professionals from a wider range of external agencies. This, in turn, will bring enhanced accountability responsibilities for SENCOs in schools.

Removing Barriers to Achievement

The government's Strategy for SEN is full of good intentions, which link closely with the Change for Children programme, as set out in *Every Child Matters*. As an action programme, RBA has already started to make steady progress in ensuring that children with less significant needs (which includes those with MLD who often have their needs overlooked in mainstream schools, and those with less severe BESD) have their needs met in a mainstream environment. The production of inclusion and SEN training materials as part of the National Primary Strategy and the Key Stage 3 Strategy has played a significant part in supporting this initiative.

The government clearly recognises that in order to enable mainstream schools to successfully include pupils with diverse needs (ASD, BESD, SLCN, SpLD and MLD) teachers will require training materials, guidance, information and access to specialist advice and support. However, irrespective of all these practical strategies, RBA also recognises that:

Table 3.1 *Removing Barriers to Achievement* – The government's strategy for SEN

Key area	Main features	SENCO role
Early intervention	Supporting early intervention; Improved information sharing between agencies; Skills and resources to take prompt action to help children falling behind peers; Provision of good-quality, accessible childcare and early years settings; Delegation of SEN funding to schools to support early intervention; Better use of ICT to enable more time to be spent with SEN pupils; Raising the skills and awareness of staff to meet the needs of SEN pupils.	**Action researcher and solution assembler** to support early identification of SEN; **Communication manager** sharing and filtering information from agencies to staff, parents, pupils; **Facilitator of personalised learning** to meet needs; **Financial manager** advising the head teacher on 'best value' for SEN provision; **Manager of SEN provision mapping** to reduce bureaucracy; **Lead professional and Leading Teacher in SEN**
Removing barriers to learning	Greater confidence to innovate; Skills and specialist support to meet SEN pupils' needs; Special and mainstream schools sharing skills and knowledge to support inclusion; Parents confident that their child's needs are met; Improved access for disabled pupils; Leadership in schools promotes inclusive practice; Residential provision reduced in special schools; Developing local communities of schools for local children; Access to study support, out-of-hours learning activities and care; Widening opportunities within the mainstream to include special school SEN pupils.	**Change agent and innovator** implementing RBA and ECM; **Manager of para-professional team** **Partnership manager** – networking, sharing expertise, skills, knowledge; **Maintenance manager** of positive relationships between parents, staff and SEN pupils; **Access manager** advising the head teacher on adaptations for disabled pupils to ensure access to curriculum, out-of-hours learning, written information and physical access; **Inclusion advocate** promoting emotional intelligence, empowering SEN pupils; creating an ethos of tolerance and acceptance of diversity; **Market researcher** surveying stakeholders' satisfaction, opinions
Raising expectations and achievement	Varied pace and approach to learning; SEN children reaching their potential Skilled and confident teachers; Practical teaching and learning resources available; Better use made of information on how well SEN pupils are progressing; Improved data on progress of SEN children who function below age-related expectations (P-scale level); More flexible, appropriate courses and curriculum matched to SEN pupils' interests and aptitudes;	**Learning facilitator** advising on learning pathways, appropriate teaching and learning approaches; **Adviser** on assessment for learning; **Training provider** to staff, parents and other professionals on SEN; **Data analyst** disseminating and using SEN data to inform provision, target setting, curriculum access and delivery; **Transition manager** for SEN pupils cross-phase, liaising with schools and other service professionals; **Pupil advocate** empowering SEN pupils, ensuring they have a part in setting their own targets, reviewing

Table 3.1 (*Continued*)

	Improved transition for SEN pupils between phases; SEN pupils given a 'voice' and more involved in decisions about their education and learning.	their own progress, and have a say in relation to their SEN provision.
Delivering improvements in partnership	Full service extended schools acting as 'hubs' for community services Proactive strategies to support child and family before crisis point reached; Multi-disciplinary integrated teams working in and around schools; Improved transparency and accountability to parents/carers; Building parents' confidence in mainstream education for SEN children; Monitoring progress and supporting improvement in school self-evaluation and regular review of effectiveness of SEN provision; Benchmarking and national data to provide comparative data on SEN performance.	**Commissioning agent** advising the head teacher on procuring services for SEN pupils to meet their needs; **Co-ordinator and manager** of para-professional team in and around school; **Parent/carers advocate** mediating, negotiating and listening to parents; **Quality assurance manager** monitoring and evaluating SEN provision in relation to 'best value' and SEN pupil outcomes (attainment, progress and achievements).

Effective inclusion relies on more than specialist skills and resources, it requires positive attitudes towards children who have difficulties in a school, a greater responsiveness to individual needs and, critically, a willingness among all staff to play their part. (DfES 2004a: 2.7)

OFSTED, in its HMI report on SEN and Disability *Towards Inclusive Schools*, acknowledged that: SENCOs identified the perceptions of staff as a major barrier to effective inclusion (OFSTED 2004a: 29).

For this very reason, SENCOs must take a proactive lead in developing the emotional intelligence of all staff within the school, including governors and non-teaching staff, such as mid-day supervisors, catering staff, site manager, administrative staff and technicians. That in itself is a huge challenge for SENCOs which needs the full support and backing of the head teacher and the governing body. The 'voice' of the SEN child and the parents/carers of that child, can contribute significantly in a whole-school staff INSET designed to help raise staff awareness about pupils' needs. Sensitive management is obviously important. An approach, which starts from the child's perspective, is extremely powerful and emotive in helping to change staff perceptions and understanding of the pupil's needs. A CD or video could be produced on a typical school day in the life of the particular child, for staff training purposes, which could be viewed as a whole staff or on an individual basis by staff and governors. The content of such an INSET session might include:

- the SEN pupil introducing themselves – nature of their special need, their age, how many in their family, how long they have had their SEN or disability, how they manage outside school, at home and in the local community;

- explanation of the barriers to learning and participation they face, from their perspective within the classroom, across the curriculum, around the school generally, on educational visits, residential experiences and in out-of-hours learning activities;
- how, from the SEN pupil's perspective, these barriers could be removed by teachers, TAs and other non-teaching staff working in various areas of the school;
- what the pupil expects generally from all staff and pupils in terms of acceptance, respect, fair treatment, reasonable adjustments, understanding and tolerance of difference and difficulties, in order to be made to feel welcome, wanted and valued as a member of the school and of the wider community, without being singled out or made to feel different from other peers and therefore more vulnerable and susceptible to bullying from others.

> *The most moving and inspiring inclusion session I ever attended was one where a young disabled student, now studying for a master's degree in law, described his educational journey through an all-age special school, sharing his frustrations and achievements with an audience of head teachers, SENCOs, advisers, education officers and consultants. The tears and laughter arising from that young man's account helped immensely to raise expectations in relation to ensuring barriers to learning and participation are removed. It also highlighted the importance of listening to the experiences and views of the young person when planning and delivering provision and co-ordinated multi-agency services for children and young people, at school and local authority level.*

It is heartening to see that the government recognises that there will always be a group of children with more complex and severe special educational needs (e.g. PMLD, SLD, BESD, ASD) who require specialist provision, and who are unable to participate full-time in a mainstream school context. However, that does not preclude them from engaging in some meaningful and relevant mainstream learning and social inclusion experiences, or from their specialist provision being co-located with a mainstream school.

Mainstream SENCOs will have an important role to play in liaising with SENCOs and inclusion managers in special schools, particularly where special school pupils are dual registered. SENCOs will need to become familiar with smaller-stepped assessment for learning (P-scales, PIVATS, B Squared, and Equals) for SEN pupils with more severe learning difficulties. In partnership with key outreach staff from the special school, the SENCO will need to ensure that all mainstream teaching and support staff working with dual-placement SEN pupils are familiar with and confident about utilising appropriate teaching strategies and assessment for learning to ensure such pupils are able to access the curriculum at the appropriate level.

Such change does not happen overnight, and there must be a realisation on behalf of senior managers in schools and among officers in local authorities that SENCOs will require the necessary non-contact time to develop valuable partnerships with the special school sector, as part of the continuum of local SEN provision, where pupils with more complex needs are being included within the mainstream. In addition, they will need quality time to work with mainstream colleagues within their own school, in order to develop their confidence, competence and capability to understand and meet the needs of a diversity of SEN pupils effectively in the mainstream classroom. RBA in relation to removing barriers to learning states:

> Inclusion is about much more than the type of school that children attend; it is about the quality of their experience; how they are helped to learn, achieve and participate fully in the life of the school. (DfES 2004a: 25)

They add:

> Schools and early years settings still vary enormously in their experience in working with children with SEN, and in the specialist expertise and resources available to them from other schools, local authority education and social services, health and voluntary organisations. *Every Child Matters* recognises the need to bring specialist services together, working in multi-disciplinary teams, to focus on the needs of the child. (ibid.: 25)

The notion of the para-professional multi-disciplinary team has echoes of the medical model, i.e. SEN pupils can only have their needs fully met, 'treated', 'cured' by the 'experts' (para-professionals), taking the onus and responsibility away from the class or subject teacher. Para-professionals may not always be teachers with SEN expertise, but also sometimes front-line workers from a range of services, including HLTAs and TAs within schools. Co-ordinating the work of a wide-ranging multi-disciplinary team will place an immense burden on the role of the SENCO, and create further complications in relation to duality of roles, if he/she happens also to be a member of the para-professional team, delivering direct services to other schools.

Despite this intention to resolve SEN pupils' difficulties via other para-professionals, it still does not get to the root cause of children and young people's barriers to achievement, which are outlined in the RBA as below:

> Difficulties in learning often arise from an unsuitable environment – inappropriate grouping of pupils, inflexible teaching styles, or inaccessible curriculum materials. (DfES 2004a: 2.1)

These barriers are largely the result of school organisational and management issues that need to be addressed by good quality leadership from the head teacher and SENCO, without making such a situation more complex and complicated by bringing in a team of para-professionals. Little consideration appears to have been given to how the SEN pupil will cope emotionally with the range of interventions from different para-professionals. The disruption to the lives of children and young people with more severe and complex needs in mainstream schools is likely to be high. Who picks up the pieces from this is likely to be the SENCO, whether or not they have been designated as the 'lead professional' co-ordinating the range of different interventions for the child. SENCOs, therefore, are likely to find they develop an enhanced counselling role for pupils facing such a situation.

Raising expectations and achievement

In relation to raising expectations and achievement, RBA has already:

- put children with SEN at the heart of personalised learning, helping schools to vary the pace of teaching to meet individual children's needs, and develop learning pathways at 14–19;
- delivered practical teaching and learning resources to raise the achievement of children with SEN through the Primary Strategy and strengthened the focus in Key Stage 3 on young people with SEN who are falling behind their peers;
- promoted and extended the use of P-scales to measure the progress made by those pupils working below level 1;
- ensured that schools get credit for the achievement of pupils with SEN (contextual value added data and point scores);
- worked with the TTA and HE sector to ensure that CPD for trainee teachers and NQTs provides a good grounding in core knowledge of SEN and that advanced and specialist skills in SEN are part of Advanced Skills and Specialist Teachers' roles and ongoing training.

SENCOs may become Advanced Skills Teachers, Excellent Teachers or Leading Teachers in SEN or BESD, with specialist skills being made available to other schools, besides their own school. In order to perform such a 'change champion' role, there has to be the guarantee that the SENCO will be able to devote two days per week to work within their own school and in other schools, and also receive their PPA time. In this situation, careful consideration will need to be given to sharing SENCO responsibilities among other staff in the school's SEN team and/or in the key stage team, Foundation stage team, or pastoral team in the secondary sector. Under the Workforce Remodelling agenda, head teachers need to give this issue some thought through the school's Change Team. It would not be recommended that head teachers take on SENCO responsibilities themselves, but to identify other respected, credible and experienced staff who could perform aspects of this role.

RBA expects those awarded Qualified Teacher Status (QTS) to demonstrate that they can:

- understand their responsibilities under the SEN Code of Practice, and know how to seek advice from specialists on less common types of SEN;
- differentiate their teaching to meet the needs of pupils, including those with SEN; and
- identify and support pupils who experience behavioural, emotional and social difficulties.

The Standards for the Induction Support Programme for those awarded QTS require:

- the head teacher to ensure that all Newly Qualified Teachers (NQTs) understand the duties and responsibilities schools have under the Disability Discrimination Act 1995 to prevent discrimination against disabled pupils;
- the Induction Tutor to arrange for NQTs to spend time with the school's SENCO to focus on specific and general SEN matters; and
- the NQT to demonstrate that they plan effectively to meet the needs of pupils in their classes with SEN, with or without statements. (DfES 2004a: 3.11)

The SENCO will have an important role to play in supporting, advising and guiding ITT trainees and NQTs on SEN and disability, and the implications for classroom practice. Where a cluster or network of schools has employed several NQTs, they may wish to collaborate and provide joint induction inputs and training on SEN. However, the SENCO in each school will need to meet with NQTs individually to discuss the individual needs of SEN pupils they teach, curriculum differentiation, IEP target-setting and implementation, and links to curriculum planning, as well as giving demonstration lessons to exemplify good inclusive practice in mainstream.

Delivering improvements in partnership

In the final chapter of RBA which focuses on delivering improvements in partnership, the government emphasises the importance of schools making inclusion an integral part of self-evaluation. This will be undertaken in terms of monitoring SEN pupil progress/outcomes in relation to:

- the types of setting in which children with SEN are taught;
- how fully SEN children are involved in the life of the school, drawing on data on admissions, attendance and exclusions, as well as about curriculum, ethos and attitudes; and
- how well SEN children achieve, including value-added measures.

As more SEN funding and resources are delegated to schools to support early intervention, accountability becomes increasingly important in order to reassure parents that they can be confident that their child with SEN is receiving the provision they need, with or without a statement, at each threshold on the SEN Code of Practice graduated approach.

RBA clarifies what information a school's SEN policy should include in order to contribute to accountability for SEN:

- how the school identifies and makes provision for children with SEN;
- the facilities the school has, including those which increase access for pupils who are disabled, including access to the curriculum;
- how resources are allocated to and among pupils with SEN;
- how the school enables pupils with SEN to engage in activities of the school together with pupils who do not have SEN;
- how the governing body evaluates the success of the school's work with pupils with SEN; and
- their arrangements for dealing with parental complaints about SEN provision. (DfES 2004a: 4.20)

SENCOs will need to focus on the further development of how they will work in partnership with the governing body (SEN governor), to evaluate the success of the school's SEN policy and provision. The DfES produced an excellent video resource (2003c), entitled: *Making a Difference*, which was a guide for SEN governors to help them clarify their role and that of the SENCO, in monitoring and evaluating school-wide SEN provision. In particular the guide points out that:

> The important thing to remember is that the SEN governor is part of a team, which consists of everyone who has responsibility for the pupils with SEN in your school. This includes other governors, the head teacher and the SENCO – in fact, the whole school staff. (DfES 2003c: 2)

It is important for the SENCO to meet regularly with the SEN governor and provide them with updates on the following information:

- how many pupils have SEN in the school;
- how many pupils are at Action, Action Plus or have a statement;
- how many staff have a role in relation to SEN and what that entails;
- how much money the school receives for pupils with SEN, how it is spent and what the impact of additional provision and interventions has on SEN pupils' outcomes (attainment and progress);
- the SEN training available to the SENCO and other staff, and how that has impacted on SEN pupils' learning, behaviour and wellbeing;
- how the school is meeting the accessibility needs of disabled pupils;
- how links with other schools (special and mainstream) are improving SEN provision; and
- how external agencies are impacting on SEN pupils' wellbeing, learning, behaviour and personal and social development.

The SENCO has to be certain that the SEN governor will keep in mind the needs of SEN pupils, especially when the governing body is considering the school budget, personnel, policies or the curriculum.

SENCOs will need to start preparing now for their future changing role, by acquiring the necessary identified continuing professional development, over the next two years, in order to equip them for this 'brave new world' and 'blue sky' thinking, which is fast becoming reality.

4

New Skills for SENCOs

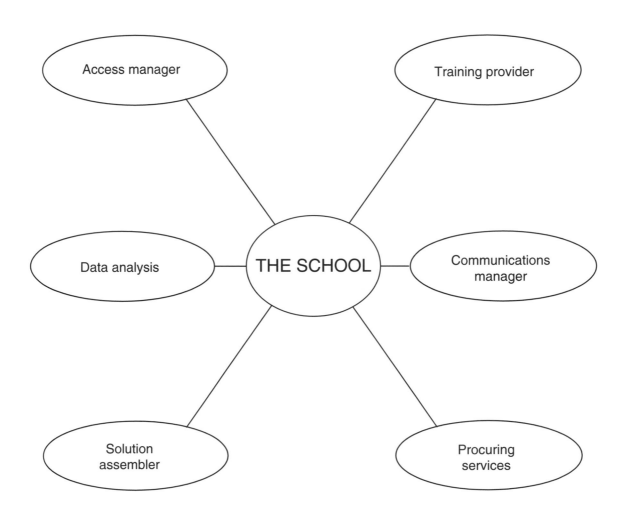

New skills for SENCOs

With the government's Change for Children programme rolling out over the next ten years, new and different skills will be required by SENCOs. The main key skills required by SENCOs are listed below:

- data analysis for value added progress
- financial management of deployment of SEN budget
- provision mapping for pupils with SEN
- procuring, brokering and commissioning services
- reducing SEN bureaucracy through the use of technology
- managing multi-agency partnerships and para-professional team
- managing communication and information sharing
- legal knowledge of SEN and disability rights
- monitoring and evaluating SEN provision
- training providing for a range of stakeholders
- inclusion facilitating for a diversity of more complex SEN pupils.

The SEN Code of Practice indicated what the role of the SENCO should be:

> The SEN Coordinator (SENCO), in collaboration with the headteacher and governing body, plays a key role in determining the strategic development of the SEN policy and provision in the school in order to raise the achievement of children with SEN. The SENCO takes responsibility for the operation of SEN policy and coordination of provision for individual children with SEN, working closely with staff, parents and carers and other agencies. The SENCO provides related professional guidance to colleagues with the aim of securing high quality teaching for children with SEN. (DfES 2001b: 5.30)

Reconceptualising the role of the SENCO

The implications of workforce remodelling, bringing in teams of para-professionals to support and deliver pupils' learning and personalised services, as well as extending the role of the Higher Level Teaching Assistant (HLTA), and the expansion of 'dawn to dusk' extended schools, all place new and extra demands on the SENCO as a strategic leader and manager of SEN throughout the school.

Robertson (2004) noted that:

> Teamwork involving SENCOs and support services (education, health and social services) is time consuming and does not always produce effective results. (Robertson 2004: 6)

The SENCO, with the support of the head teacher, is going to be a significant and crucial key player in moving this radical educational agenda forward. SENCOs' increased strategic leadership role clearly necessitates senior management status as of right and a much needed revision and updating of the original TTA National Standards for SENCOs.

The DfES revised the National Standards for Headteachers in October 2004, and these appear to be far more relevant and appropriate to the new role for SENCOs, working in schools of the future. These particular standards were updated in recognition of the changing role of headship required in the twenty-first century, in order to further develop and deliver the government's educational change programme. They cover six key areas:

- Shaping the future
- Leading learning and teaching

- Developing self and working with others
- Managing the organisation
- Securing accountability
- Strengthening community.

Within each of the six key areas, the knowledge requirements, professional qualities – i.e. the skills, dispositions and personal capabilities – and the actions needed to achieve the core purpose are identified.

The intention in this chapter is to remodel and realign the original SENCO Standards with the six key areas in the revised National Standards for Headteachers, which more realistically reflect the evolving SENCO role in order to meet the challenges and opportunities of *Every Child Matters*, and *Removing the Barriers to Achievement* in schools. The remodelled SENCO standards will help to provide a framework for professional development.

The remodelled SENCO Standards are set out in the form of an audit, to enable SENCOs to identify aspects of their new role that will require further professional development.

Table 4.1 Audit for new SENCO role

Indicate how confident you are about the aspects of each dimension by rating your skill confidence level on a scale of 1–3 (1 = not yet acquired; 2 = developing; 3 = securely in place)

1. Shaping the future	Rating
● Knowledge of local, national and global trends in SEN, applying relevant evidence to shape SEN provision	☐
● Build and communicate a coherent whole school vision for SEN which helps to develop a positive inclusive ethos	☐
● Demonstrate the SEN vision and values in everyday work and practice through motivating and working with others	☐
● Think and plan strategically for SEN whole school, to take account of the diversity, values and experience of the school and the local community	☐
● Set standards and provide examples of best practice for other teachers in identifying, assessing and meeting the needs of SEN pupils	☐
● Ensure creativity, innovation and the use of appropriate new technologies to achieve excellence in SEN	☐
● Translate SEN vision and SEN policy into agreed objectives and priorities for operational plans	☐
● Set realistic but challenging goals and targets for SEN with the head teacher, which improve and sustain high standards in SEN pupil achievement and wellbeing	☐
● Effectively communicate SEN policy and provision within and beyond the school to the local authority, external agencies, parents and carers, pupils, other schools, colleges	☐

2. Leading learning and teaching	
● Ensure that learning is at the centre of strategic planning and resource management for SEN (provision mapping)	☐
● Ensure a culture and ethos where SEN pupils achieve success and become engaged in their own learning	☐
● Demonstrate and articulate high expectations for SEN pupils and set stretching targets for SEN	☐
● Demonstrate the principles and practice of effective teaching and learning for SEN pupils	☐
● Promote the development of a personalised learning culture for SEN pupils	☐
● Support the implementation of flexible learning curriculum pathways to remove barriers to achievement	☐
● Support the use of effective appropriate graduated curriculum assessment for learning for SEN pupils	☐

(*Continued*)

Table 4.1 (*Continued*)

- Support the capacity building of other staff (teachers and teaching assistants), to meet the needs of SEN pupils effectively, by ensuring they understand the learning needs of SEN pupils ☐
- Support curriculum differentiation and teacher planning (personalisation) to ensure access and participation for pupils with SEN and disability ☐
- Know about and support the implementation of effective strategies which secure high standards of behaviour and attendance among SEN pupils ☐
- Support the development of improvement in SEN pupils' basic skills in literacy, numeracy, ICT and in study skills, in order to improve access to the wider curriculum and out-of-hours learning activities ☐
- Lead and develop effective liaison between schools and colleges cross-phase, to ensure continuity and progression in SEN pupils' learning ☐
- Help to address SEN pupils' achievement by collecting, analysing and disseminating SEN pupil performance data to other staff, in order to establish benchmarks, inform SEN provision, curriculum access and delivery, and SEN target-setting processes at individual pupil and whole-school level ☐
- Interpret relevant national and local SEN data and inspection evidence, and compare with school SEN performance ☐
- Monitor, evaluate and review the teaching, learning and support SEN pupils receive, and recommend strategies to remove barriers to achievement ☐
- Promote the use of new and emerging technologies to enhance and extend the learning experiences of SEN pupils ☐

3. Developing self and working with others

- Judge when to make decisions and when to consult with others, including external agencies ☐
- Manage own workload and time effectively to allow for an appropriate work/life balance ☐
- Take responsibility for own professional development ☐
- Encourage all staff to recognise and fulfil their statutory responsibilities to pupils with SEN and disability ☐
- Support staff by ensuring that all involved have the necessary information to secure improvements in teaching and learning, and disseminate good practice in SEN across the school ☐
- Ensure effective planning, allocation, support and evaluation of work undertaken by staff in the SEN/para-professional team ☐
- Ensure clear delegation of tasks and devolution of appropriate SEN responsibilities ☐
- Give and receive effective feedback and act to improve personal performance ☐
- Know about strategies to promote individual and team development for SEN ☐
- Advise, contribute to and co-ordinate the professional development of staff to increase their effectiveness in responding to the needs of pupils with SEN ☐
- Provide support and training to trainee and NQTs in relation to understanding the needs of SEN pupils, and raising their achievement and attainment ☐
- Support staff in developing constructive working relationships with SEN pupils and their parents/carers ☐
- Develop and maintain a culture of high expectations for self and others working in the SEN team, and take appropriate action when performance is unsatisfactory ☐
- Accept support from others including colleagues, governors, the local authority and external agencies in relation to SEN policy, practice and provision ☐
- Collaborate and network with other SENCOs and SEN professionals within and beyond the school ☐
- Manage conflict and tensions within the SEN team ☐

4. Managing the organisation of SEN

- Know the principles, strategies and models of school self-evaluation and school improvement for SEN ☐
- Produce and implement a clear, evidence-based development plan and policy for SEN ☐
- Ensure that SEN policy and practice takes account of national and local circumstances, policies, initiatives and strategies ☐
- Know the principles of strategic financial planning, budgetary management and best value in relation to planning and procuring SEN provision and services ☐
- Know the principles and process of managing change in relation to SEN whole school ☐

Table 4.1 (*Continued*)

- Understand the legislation relating to SEN, Disability, Safeguarding Children, Equal Opportunities, Human Rights, Race Relations, and Health and Safety ☐
- Use new and emerging technologies (ICT) to enhance the organisational effectiveness and management of SEN within the school ☐
- Manage the organisation of SEN efficiently and effectively on a day-to-day basis ☐
- Prioritise, plan and organise self and others in the SEN team ☐
- Manage the deployment of SEN financial and human resources effectively and efficiently (provision map), to achieve the educational goals and priorities for SEN ☐
- Manage and organise the SEN resource base learning environment efficiently and effectively to ensure that it meets the needs of the curriculum and health and safety regulations ☐
- Ensure that the range, quality and use of all available resources for SEN is monitored, evaluated and reviewed to improve the quality of education for all SEN pupils, to provide value for money ☐
- Maintain existing resources for SEN and explore opportunities to develop or incorporate new resources from a wide range of sources inside and outside the school, within the local community ☐
- Think creatively to anticipate and solve SEN problems ☐
- Make professional, managerial and organisational decisions about SEN policy and provision, based on informed judgements ☐
- Implement successful performance management and appraisal processes with staff in the SEN team ☐
- Monitor the implementation of delegated management tasks for SEN ☐

5. Securing accountability

- Know the key educational frameworks for SEN and disability ☐
- Have knowledge of accountability frameworks in relation to multi-agency service delivery for SEN provision ☐
- Understand the principles and practice of quality assurance systems for SEN, including school self-evaluation, school improvement processes ☐
- Collect, analyse and use a rich set of SEN data to monitor, evaluate, understand and identify trends, strengths and weaknesses of SEN policy and provision to inform improvement ☐
- Work with the governing body (SEN governor), to provide information, objective advice and support in relation to SEN, in order to enable them to meet their SEN responsibilities ☐
- Develop and present a coherent, understandable and accurate account of the school's performance in SEN to a range of audiences within and outside the school ☐
- Reflect on personal contribution made to whole-school achievements in SEN and take account of feedback from others ☐

6. Strengthening community

- Know about the rich and diverse resources existing within the local community that can enhance SEN pupils' learning ☐
- Have knowledge of the roles and work of other agencies (health, social services, education and voluntary organisations) working with SEN pupils ☐
- Develop effective liaison with external agencies in order to provide maximum support for SEN pupils ☐
- Co-operate and work collaboratively in partnership with relevant agencies to safeguard and promote the wellbeing of SEN children ☐
- Demonstrate commitment to effective team work within the school and with external agencies in relation to SEN ☐
- Collaborate and network with other schools (mainstream and special) to share best SEN practice, promote innovative SEN initiatives and improve SEN outcomes ☐
- Build and maintain effective relationships with parents and carers, partners and the community, that enhance the education of SEN pupils ☐
- Listen to, reflect and act on community feedback in relation to SEN policy and provision ☐
- Ensure learning experiences for SEN pupils are linked into and integrated with the wider community ☐
- Create and maintain an effective partnership with parents and carers to support and improve their SEN child's learning, achievements and personal development ☐

- Communicate effectively with parents and carers to provide information about their child's targets, achievements and progress ☐
- Develop and maintain effective partnerships between parents/carers and the school's staff so as to promote SEN pupils' learning ☐
- Listen to and seek information from parents and carers about their child's special educational needs and disability ☐
- Seek opportunities to enhance and enrich the school's provision for SEN from the local community ☐

(Adapted from DfES 2004j; *National Standards for Headteachers*)

5

SENCOs and the New Relationship with Schools

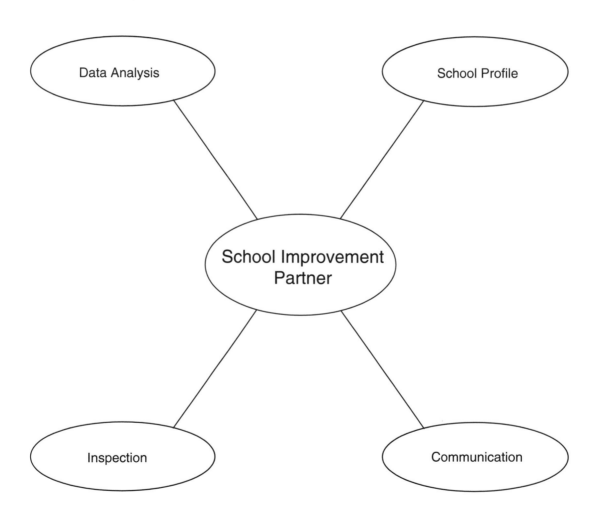

Table 5.1 Components of the New Relationship with Schools process

NETWORKING AND COLLABORATION

CHALLENGE			SUPPORT
	Communication	Data	School Self-evaluation
		Single conversation	
	School Improvement Partner	School profile	Inspection

TRUST

Definition of a new relationship with schools

The New Relationship with Schools (NRwS) is the relationship between self-evaluation and school improvement. It adopts a more simplified approach to school improvement, in an attempt to reduce bureaucracy, while ensuring that every child matters.

School Improvement Partner and the single conversation

The School Improvement Partner (SIP) can be a serving head teacher, a recently serving head teacher, consultant/seconded head teacher or a local authority link adviser/attached inspector for the school.

The SIP leads the annual single conversation, which is a focused dialogue with the head teacher, about how well the school is performing and its priorities for the future. The SIP will pose questions, suggest sources of evidence, challenge interpretations of the school's evidence, discuss the accuracy of the head teacher's improvement priorities and act as a critical reader of the school's self-evaluation form (SEF).

The SIP will consider the support a school draws upon from its various partnerships, and what contribution the school makes to the local learning community. In addition, the SIP has a role in enabling schools to share their best practice across the system, within and beyond the school. They also sign off the school improvement grants.

The school profile

The annual school profile (introduced 2005/6) aims to capture the richness of school performance in a way that is jargon-free, user-friendly, easy to access and powerful in impact. It provides a rounded account of what the school offers its pupils and its community, combining centrally generated data with the school's own narrative. It provides parents with a broader and deeper understanding of what the school is doing. The school profile will support more intelligent accountability for the full range of what schools do for every child, including more personalised learning. The profile will also promote the emphasis in *Every Child Matters* on the need to support all children to develop their full potential. The school profile encourages an inclusive approach, by showing how the school serves the full range of their pupils, i.e. how staff help

Table 5.2 New Relationships with Schools single conversation process

Inputs	Focus of the Single Conversation	Outputs
■ School's self-evaluation linked to OFSTED self-evaluation form (SEF) ■ Inspection evidence ■ School's development plan ■ National and local authority priorities ■ Improvement grant, value for money comparisons ■ Data on pupil wellbeing ■ Exceptions report on pupil attainment and equity gaps (school improvement data), benchmarking data – contextual value added	1. Standards of achievement, attendance and behaviour 2. Challenge and support for 'bottom-up' targets – agreeing targets 3. Moderate the school's self-evaluation process (SEF) 4. Agree priorities for future improvement 5. Identify action and external support for improvement 6. Sign off the School Improvement Grant 7. Consideration of the School's Profile 8. Consideration of networks and links with other schools and agencies 9. Head teacher's performance and the school's performance management systems *Key questions:* **How well is the school performing?** **What are the key factors?** **What are the key priorities?** **How will the school achieve them?**	■ Improved analysis, better planning, reduced bureaucracy ■ Report to head, governors, LA, (DfES for Academies) on: – self-assessment – priorities and targets – action – package of support including engagement with other schools ■ Recommendation on specialist schools re-designation ■ Advice to governing body on head's performance management and school's performance management systems

(Adapted from DfES/OFSTED 2005, *A New Relationship with Schools: Next Steps*, page 24)

pupils achieve their full potential, the ways in which they support pupils and what they are trying to improve. It replaces the annual report to parents; it complements performance tables and increases the flexibility around elements of the school prospectus.

Members of the governing body are responsible for signing off the profile. The profile should be in A4 format, relatively short (between two and four pages) and allow for easy comparisons between schools. It is compiled and accessed electronically, on-line, and can be viewed on TeacherNet, GovernorsNet and the DfES Parents Centre.

The school profile contains the following information:

- data on pupils' attainment and progress, set against benchmarks for schools in similar contexts;
- how the school serves all its pupils;
- the most recent assessment by OFSTED, set against the school's own self-assessment;
- what the school offers, in terms of the broader curriculum, including extra-curricular activities;
- the school's priorities for future improvement;
- what the school offers to the wider community;
- other information, including contextual information about the school, e.g. free school meals (FSM), SEN, exclusion rates, attendance, religious denominations, pupil destinations.

The school profile gives a school the opportunity to describe:

- its successes and plans for the future;
- the curriculum and activities beyond the curriculum;
- how the school helps every pupil achieve their full potential;
- how the school is engaging with the wider community, including parents/carers and other schools; and
- what has been done in response to the latest inspection.

Communication

Streamlining communication with schools in order to help reduce bureaucracy and support professional development is another feature of the New Relationship with Schools. Web integration (integration of all the DfES's school websites) and on-line ordering of DfES publications in response to a fortnightly e-mail, replaces the monthly 'paper batch' of documentation sent to schools. This will enable schools to choose what they want to receive and when they want to receive it. The launch of Teachers' TV, featuring programmes on training and development, classroom resources and education news, has supported the ongoing professional development of teachers.

Data for school improvement

The Exceptions Report uses Fischer Family Trust (FFT) data and contextualised value-added data to inform the School Improvement Partner (SIP) and the school. The report covers social deprivation, mobility, date of birth within year, gender, ethnicity and SEN. Integration of the Pupil Achievement Tracker (PAT) and OFSTED Performance and Assessment Reports (PANDA) into a single electronic system facilitates data analysis and the identification of trends. The data analysis focuses on three key areas:

- the overall standards pupils attain and the standards attained by different groups, i.e. girls, boys, gifted and talented, children in public care, those from different ethnic groups, those with a diversity of SEN and disability;
- the progress made by pupils over time, i.e. how well pupils do between entering nursery and leaving the Foundation Stage, or between KS2 and KS4, or over all key stages;
- the progress pupils make in their personal development and wellbeing, including the five outcomes of *Every Child Matters*.

Data analysis on attendance, exclusions and pupil destinations will contribute to judgements in relation to *Every Child Matters* outcomes, along with inspection outcomes and school self-evaluation evidence on pupil outcomes, especially in relation to health, behaviour, attendance and engagement.

Inspection

Changes in OFSTED inspections of schools:

- based on school self-evaluation evidence;
- shorter notice of inspection, i.e. two to five days;
- smaller inspection team with HMI involved in and leading the inspection;
- inspection team in the school for two days;
- inspection process will entail discussions with staff, pupils; scrutiny of written work; examination of data and assessment records; tracking pupils through a school day will be more prominent than inspection of subjects;

- inspection covers the four key areas: quality of education provided; educational standards achieved; leadership and management; spiritual, moral, social and cultural development (pupils' wellbeing linked to the five outcomes of *Every Child Matters*);
- three-year interval between inspections;
- inspection reports shorter, between four and six pages in length, more readable for parents, reporting on pupils' views, focus on outcomes, quality and impact of leadership and management, clearer recommendations for improvement made;
- judgement criteria on a scale of 1 to 4 (1 = outstanding, 2 = good, 3 = satisfactory and 4 = inadequate);
- two categories of schools causing concern:
  - (a) special measures, where the school is failing to provide an adequate standard of education and has insufficient capacity to improve;
  - (b) notice to improve, where the school is not performing as well as it should in one or more respect but provides an acceptable education.

School self-evaluation

A continuous activity that is at the heart of the school improvement process. School self-evaluation is based on a rigorous and honest analysis of evidence, which includes the views of parents and pupils.

Rigorous self-evaluation helps schools to improve. It needs to be manageable, comprehensive and integrated readily with routine management systems. Self-evaluation should enable schools to listen to, and do something about, the views of their stakeholders, parents and pupils. It should be an annual process, where the self-evaluation form (SEF) is updated, and includes information about the impact of its action on learners.

In order to ensure effective self-evaluation, schools need to provide sufficient evidence in response to each question below:

- Does the self-evaluation identify how well the school serves its learners?
- How does the school compare with the best schools, and the best comparable schools?
- Is the self-evaluation integral to the school's key management systems?
- Is the school's self-evaluation based on a good range of telling evidence? For example, this should include external evidence, i.e. evaluating the impact of extended services, including daycare, on the learning and wellbeing of learners; reports from the school community and external agencies involved in the work of the school and with individual learners.
- Does the self-evaluation and planning involve key people in the school and seek the views of parents, learners and external advisers and agencies? For example, is the self-evaluation undertaken systematically at all levels, e.g. subject leaders, SENCO?
- Does the self-evaluation lead to action to achieve the school's longer-term goals for development?

SENCOs applying the New Relationship with Schools process

SENCOs leading SEN strategically within their school would be well advised to adopt and utilise the New Relationship with Schools (NRwS) model. This process would help to strengthen considerably the monitoring and evaluation of SEN policy and provision, whole-school, through the involvement of an external partner, and with the support of the head teacher.

Taking key components of NRwS, examples of how SENCOs can apply the process to SEN will be explained in more detail. While there is no compulsion for SENCOs to adopt the NRwS model for SEN, it is recommended best practice for those SENCOs who are likely to work in an extended full-service school.

School Improvement Partner and the Single Conversation for SEN

The School Improvement Partner (SIP) for the SENCO would ideally be an experienced and lead SENCO from another school, or the local authority SEN adviser, or external SEN Consultant.

The Single Conversation with the external partner would be based on similar lines to that of the head teacher's, and be related specifically to SEN.

Ideally, the Single Conversation related to SEN would focus on the following:

- How have you addressed the issues for improvement in SEN, which were identified from the previous inspection?
- How well does the school perform in relation to SEN overall?
- What are the strengths and best practice in SEN within the school?
- What is the SEN data telling you about standards? Are there any surprises?
- Are there any trends or issues identified from your SEN data analysis that require further attention? If so, how do you intend to move forward on addressing these?
- What is the correlation between contextual factors and SEN pupils' attainment, progress and achievements in relation to learning, behaviour and wellbeing? For example, how many pupils with poor attendance or who have been excluded, or are in public care or have SEN?
- Have you met all the targets, priorities and actions for SEN on your development plan? If not, what barriers have prevented you from meeting all the targets set?
- How have you engaged with other key staff within school in monitoring and evaluating attainment and progress for pupils with SEN?
- What impact has the additional SEN provision delivered by staff within the school had on SEN pupils' outcomes, e.g. attainment, progress, achievements in relation to learning, behaviour and wellbeing?
- What impact has the support, advice, guidance and interventions provided by professionals from external multi-disciplinary agencies had on SEN pupils' outcomes?
- How have you monitored and evaluated the SEN budget and the SEN provision to ensure value for money?
- How have you ensured that reasonable adjustments for disabled pupils have been made in order to ensure that they receive full access to buildings, classrooms, facilities; access to the curriculum, out-of-hours learning activities, school residential experiences and educational visits; and access to written information in alternative formats?
- What would you wish to include or add to the School's Profile for SEN?
- How have you ensured that all staff are implementing the five outcomes for children as set out in *Every Child Matters*?
- What are your future priorities for SEN provision that you wish to target for improvement?
- What further internal or external advice, guidance, support or training would you value in order to assist you in your role as SENCO?

SEN data analysis and school improvement

OFSTED noted from their inspection findings nationally, that:

> The availability and use of data on outcomes for pupils with SEN continues to be limited. (OFSTED 2004a: 5)

and:

> The quality of provision for low-attaining groups and its effect on achievement and self-esteem is seldom well enough assessed. (ibid.: 80.17–18)

Individual pupil progress and achievement data are at the heart of school improvement and inclusion. The National Primary Strategy and the Key Stage 3 Strategy (now the Secondary Strategy) have produced excellent resources to support SENCOs in analysing and using data to raise the attainment of SEN pupils, in self-evaluating SEN provision and in mapping and planning SEN provision.

Although all teachers need to be involved in data analysis, the assessment co-ordinator, subject leaders, key stage co-ordinators and strategy managers in schools, in particular, have a key role to play with the SENCO in judging standards and rates of progress of SEN pupils. Data analysis helps to improve teaching and learning and also supports the target-setting process, at whole-school and at individual pupil level. The SENCO can also enable the school leadership team to make appropriate strategic decisions about SEN provision whole-school, on the basis of thorough in-depth SEN data analysis.

OFSTED noted:

> In schools that were most successful with pupils with SEN, systems for assessment and planning were fully integrated with those for other pupils. This helped to ensure that planning for pupils with SEN was done by all staff and not only by SEN teachers as a separate exercise. (OFSTED 2004a: 48)

Any SEN pupil data analysis must address the essential school improvement questions:

- How well is the school doing in relation to SEN?
- How does the school's SEN standards and provision compare with similar schools?
- How well should the school be doing in relation to SEN?
- What can be achieved in SEN next year?
- What has to be done to make the SEN improvement happen?

Thorough interrogation of SEN data leads SENCOs to seek answers to the following questions:

- Why are some SEN pupils underachieving? For example:
    1. achieving below levels 1 and 2 at the end of Key Stage 1;
    2. achieving below level 3 at the end of Key Stage 2;
    3. are not moving and are stuck at levels 3 or 4 at the end of Key Stage 3, i.e. the same levels with which they entered Year 7, bearing in mind that the expectation is that the majority of pupils with SEN will make at least one level of progress across the three years of Key Stage 3 in the core subjects of the National Curriculum.
- Are teachers' expectations high enough?
- Has a wide range of appropriate teaching strategies been used across the curriculum?
- Have appropriate methods of assessment, which are smaller stepped, been utilised for pupils with learning difficulties?
- Are there factors external to school, that are creating a barrier to pupils' learning, and thus resulting in underachievement?
- Could more be done to support SEN pupils' learning beyond school hours at home, e.g. e-learning, using ICT?
- Have appropriate additional Wave 2 and 3 interventions been utilised?

OFSTED commented:

> Until more is expected from the lowest-attaining pupils, improvement in provision for pupils with SEN and in standards they reach will continue to be slow. (OFSTED 2004a: 111.23)

Further questions for SENCOs in relation to data analysis:

- What data would be useful to collect in relation to recording SEN pupils' progress in wellbeing?
- How could the QCA EBD scale be utilised to show value-added progress in relation to targeted pupils' learning, conduct and emotional behaviour?
- How often and when should SEN data be used in school?
- How can SEN data be produced in more interesting, meaningful and user-friendly formats for governors, parents, staff and pupils?
- How can parents/carers become more familiar with the smaller-stepped assessment used for their child with special educational needs, e.g. P-scales, PIVATS, B Squared, Equals?
- How could the local special school support SEN data analysis?

Pupil Achievement Tracker (PAT)

The assessment co-ordinator in school will be familiar with using the Pupil Achievement Tracker (PAT) and can support the SENCO in interrogating SEN data. PAT is an analytical information software package that will enable the SENCO to make judgements about whether SEN pupils make sufficient progress in relation to their prior attainment. Other contextual factors are also included such as: ethnicity, gender, transience/mobility, social deprivation, date of birth in relation to Year group, SEN Code of Practice graduated response threshold, category of SEN according to the Pupil Level Annual Schools Census (PLASC), and interventions used. PAT can record statutory key stage data and optional QCA test and teacher assessment data, in addition to P-scale data. Data have to be imported into PAT from the school's management information system. PAT provides value-added line graphs and progress charts.

The performance data to enhance annual school performance profiles is shown in the chart below. This can contribute to the school's profile, particularly if the SENCO produces an additional SEN school profile.

Value added progress

'Value added' is a term frequently referred to in relation to progress made by pupils. Value-added progress looks at rates of progress over time in addition to attainment. There is an assumption that prior attainment is correlated with later attainment for pupils. Value-added measures use point scores, which convert P-scales and National Curriculum levels to number equivalents.

OFSTED uses point scores in their Performance and Assessment Reports (PANDA). Performance tables also utilise point scores, which provide a more inclusive measure, ensuring that every child's progress is recognised by a point score equivalent, however small that progress may be. When SENCOs track SEN pupil progress, it is often useful to record this progress using point scores.

A pupil's value-added score is the difference between their predicted and their actual result. One value-added point is equivalent to one-sixth of a level, or one term's progress. The minimum expected point score gain for a pupil is three points per year. This should enable SENCOs to obtain a benchmark in relation to SEN pupil progress over an academic year.

Table 5.3 Additional indicators for schools (Source: DfES 2004b)

Indicators that may be used to help evaluate performance regarding the inclusion and attainment of pupils with SEN	Source
For children working at P-scales: increase in points score between key stages	School return/Local indicator
Percentage of pupils achieving below Level 3 at Key Stage 2 (English and Maths) compared with benchmark group excluding complex needs and EAL stages 1, 2 and 3	Filtered PAT data
Number of children excluded on fixed-term basis	School/LA data
Number of episodes of exclusion on fixed-term basis (children excluded one or more times in academic year)	School/LA data
% Attendance: primary/secondary by academic year	School/LA data
Number of children with Pastoral Support Plans	School data
Number of children in public care with Personal Education Plans	School data
Number of pupils on roll and attending 80% or more for 12 months and who were previously subject to exclusion (all types) from elsewhere	School data (match to children in public care)
Number of children of statutory school age on part-time timetables	School data
Number of children attending part-time but on the roll of other specialist provision	School data
Number of children transferred to specialist provision over academic year (school or unit)	School data
Number of children taken onto roll during the year who were previously registered in special school or unit provision	School data
Percentage of catchment area population who attend a special school or rate per 1,000	School data
Number of children with identified special educational needs at School Action Plus	PLASC
Number of children on roll and holding statements	PLASC
% Annual Reviews completed on time in academic year	LA data
Number of statements discontinued in academic year	SEN Form 2
Number of requests for Statutory assessment during academic year	SEN Form 2
Number of new statements during academic year	SEN Form 2
For Special Schools – number of children on roll but attending mainstream part-time (year on year data)	LA data
For Special Schools – number of children on roll but attending mainstream full-time (year on year data)	School data

Table 5.4 Examples of point score equivalents for P-scales and NC levels

P3 = 1 P4 = 1.5 P5 = 2 P6 = 2.5 P7 = 3 P8 = 5
(These equivalent point scores for P-scales are from Lancashire LEA PIVATS)

W (working towards) = 3
Level 1c = 7 Level 1b = 9 Level 1a = 11
Level 2c = 13 Level 2b = 15 Level 2a = 17
Level 3c = 19 Level 3b = 21 Level 3a = 23
Level 4c = 25 Level 4b = 27 Level 4a = 29
Level 5 = 33
Level 6 = 39

GCSE points: A* = 8 A = 7 B = 6 C = 5 D = 4 E = 3 F = 2 G = 1
Short GCSE points: A* = 4 A = 3.5 B = 3 C = 2.5 D = 2 E = 1.5 F = 1 G = 0.5

GNVQ Full Intermediate: Pass = 20 Merit = 24 Distinction = 30
GNVQ Full Foundation: Pass = 6 Merit = 12 Distinction = 16

Contextual value added

This compares the progress made by each pupil with the average progress made by similar pupils in similar schools.

Self-evaluation and SEN

Evaluation of the effectiveness of SEN provision is an integral and essential part of school self-evaluation. Local authorities usually provide schools with a locally agreed framework for evaluation, which is more than likely to be aligned with the OFSTED framework for self-evaluation. An example of a self-evaluation and monitoring framework that SENCOs could utilise, which is aligned with the five outcomes of *Every Child Matters*, can be found at the end of Chapter 6, and on the accompanying CD.

According to the DfES (2004b), in their guidance on the management of SEN expenditure, any local authority self-evaluation scheme for SEN should:

- build on the school's self-evaluation of what it achieves for all its pupils, by evaluating specific aspects of provision for pupils with SEN;
- be based on a locally agreed mechanism that allows the school and the local authority to arrive at a shared view of the school's effectiveness – so as to avoid duplication of school self-evaluation and local authority monitoring processes;
- form part of the school's regular cycle of self evaluation, and support the process of providing information for the purposes of OFSTED inspection;
- be based on agreed outcome measures that enable the school to compare the effectiveness of its provision for pupils with SEN, with that achieved by similar schools;
- include outcome measures related to pupil attainment, social and emotional development and social inclusion, and achievement in its wider sense, i.e. wellbeing (*Every Child Matters* five outcomes for children);
- in focusing on outcomes for pupils in the school, address also the issue of admissions (pupils in the school's catchment area who for whatever reason do not attend the school);
- be informed by the views of everyone in the school community: pupils, parents, governors and staff;
- identify effective practice that can be celebrated and shared within and beyond the school;
- help the school know what it needs to do next to improve outcomes, and lead naturally into action planning;
- be accessible and easy to use.

(DfES 2004b: 19–20)

The National Service Framework for Children, Young People and Maternity Services and the link to school self-evaluation

The National Service Framework (NSF) is integral to the implementation of the Children Act 2004 and local change programmes. It comprises 11 quality standards for health, social care and some education services, to be implemented over the next ten years, for children and young people under 19.

The first five universal standards are for all children and young people. The next five standards (Ss 6 to 10) cover services for children and young people requiring more specialised care, treatment and support, and the final standard (S 11), is for pregnant women and their partners (see pp. 53–5, Table 5.5)

The NSF Standards aim to ensure high-quality and integrated health and social care from pregnancy through to adulthood. They ensure that services and personalised care are designed and delivered around the needs of the child. They support a holistic child-centred approach, whereby not just the illness or the problem are looked at, but the best ways to pick up problems early, take preventative action and ensure children have the best possible chance to realise their full potential are considered.

Professionals and practitioners from health, social services and education work together in partnership to provided joined-up co-ordinated services. Following the NSF will help these professionals to raise standards in hospitals, GP surgeries, schools and nurseries, maternity units and Sure Start children's centres.

The evidence-based standards will feed into the new integrated inspection framework; they will support school and service self-evaluation and they will align closely to the *Every Child Matters: Change for Children* programme, in order to improve outcomes for children and young people.

The NSF standards will ensure that services for children, young people and their families are:

- quicker and easier to use;
- better at giving children, young people and their parents/carers increased information, power and choice over their care;
- more closely matched to individual children and young people's needs;
- better co-ordinated so not too many professionals are seen by the child;
- better at achieving good results for children and young people;
- better at involving children, young people and families in decisions about their care and wellbeing;
- more like what children and young people say they want; and
- able to safeguard and promote the welfare of children and young people.

How SENCOs can utilise the National Service Framework standards

Some of the standards, particularly Standards 5, 8, 9 and 10, will have greater relevance to school settings. SENCOs will need to ensure that when they self-evaluate SEN policy and provision – which includes services delivered within the school by external professionals from health, social services and education – they refer to the relevant NSF standard descriptor, to judge if it has been met.

The NSF is supported by exemplar materials illustrating key themes in the standards, which can be used for multi-disciplinary training at local authority level. They can be used by SENCOs and head teachers at school level, to support school self-review and school improvement, through the New Relationship with Schools process. They can also be used by clusters or networks of schools to focus on a shared common issue, for example, cross-phase transition and multi-agency service delivery to schools. This practice supports the government's SEN strategy, *Removing Barriers to Achievement*, in relation to area 4: delivering improvements in partnership. Two exemplars, in particular, will be of interest to SENCOs: Asthma and Autism Spectrum Disorders (ASD).

The ASD exemplar illustrates how the standards in the NSF can be met by schools and agencies working in partnership to support the child on their 'journey' from initial identification, through early childhood, to 16 and beyond school into early adulthood (up to 19). It provides helpful cross-referencing for each action to the relevant NSF standard. It also provides clear examples of the successful integration of children's services through the use of a common assessment framework and multi-disciplinary service teams working together.

The exemplars may be useful to:

- provide a 'benchmark' for the quality of multi-agency involvement;
- highlight further references and key clinical guidelines;
- stimulate local debate in clusters and networks to assist multi-agency partners to re-evaluate the way they collaborate on, commission and deliver children's services;
- provide a multi-disciplinary training tool for staff working with children and young people to raise awareness of specific issues, and stimulate discussion;
- canvas the views of 'users' (children, young people and their parents/carers), through focus groups, on the quality and effectiveness of service delivery;
- enable the SENCO, using a case study approach with colleagues within the school, in partnership with external professionals from health, social services and education, to map the similarities and differences in the 'journey' of a similar pupil with, for example, ASD in their school.

Table 5.5 At-a-glance summary of the National Service Framework standards for children, young people and maternity services

Standard title	Standard descriptor	Main themes in Standard
1. **Promoting health and wellbeing, identifying needs and intervening early**	The health and wellbeing of all children and young people is promoted and delivered through a co-ordinated programme of action, including prevention and early intervention wherever possible, to ensure long-term gain led by the NHS in partnership with local authorities	Child Health Programme to reduce health inequalities. Multi-agency health promotion. Healthy lifestyles promoted. Universal and targeted health promotion. Access to targeted services. Early intervention and assessing needs.
2. **Supporting parenting**	Parents and carers are enabled to receive the information, services and support which will help them to care for their children and equip them with the skills they need to ensure that their children have optimum life chances and are healthy and safe	Universal, targeted and specialist services to support mothers and fathers. Up-to-date information and education for parents. Support for parents of preschool children to help children develop secure attachments and to develop. Support for parents of school-aged children to involve them in their child's learning and behaviour management. Early, multi-agency support for parents with specific needs, i.e. mental health problems, addiction to drugs, alcohol; parents of disabled children, teenage parents. Co-ordinated services across child and adult services. Multi-disciplinary support to meet the needs of adoptive parents/adults caring for looked-after children.
3. **Child, young person and family-centred services**	Children and young people and families receive high-quality services which are co-ordinated around their individual and family needs and take account of their views	Appropriate information to children, young people and their parents. Listening and responding to them in relation to their care and treatment. Services respectful to the wishes of children and young people. Improved access to services. Robust multi-agency planning and commissioning arrangements, i.e. Children's Trusts, Common Assessment Framework. Quality and safety of care in delivering of child-centred services.

(Continued)

Table 5.5 (*Continued*)

Standard title	Standard descriptor	Main themes in Standard
		Common core of skills, knowledge and competencies for staff working with children and young people, across all agencies.
4. Growing up into adulthood	All young people have access to age-appropriate services which are responsive to their specific needs as they grow into adulthood	Confidentiality and consent for young people. Health promotion to meet needs, i.e. reduce teenage pregnancy, smoking, substance misuse, suicide, sexually transmitted infections. Support achievement of full potential, e.g. Connexions and Youth Services. Improved access to services and advice for those who are disabled, in special circumstances or who live in rural areas. Transition to full adult services. Additional support available for looked-after children leaving care and other young people in special circumstances.
5. Safeguarding and promoting the welfare of children and young people	All agencies work to prevent children suffering harm and to promote their welfare, provide them with the services they require to address their identified needs and safeguard children who are being or who are likely to be harmed	All agencies prioritise safeguarding and promoting the welfare of children. LA children and Young People's Plan. Clarification of agencies' roles and responsibilities. Profile of local population to identify and assess vulnerable children. High-quality integrated services to meet needs of children at risk of harm, abused or neglected. Effective supervision for staff working with children to ensure clear, accurate, comprehensive, up-to-date records are kept, and high-quality services delivered.
6. Children and young people who are ill	All children and young people who are ill or thought to be ill or injured will have timely access to appropriate advice and to effective services which address their health, social, educational and emotional needs throughout the period of their illness	Comprehensive, integrated, timely local services. Professionals support children, young people and their families in self-care of their illness. Access to advice and services in a range of settings. Trained, competent professionals providing consistent advice to assist and treat a child who is ill. High-quality treatment, and high-quality care for those with long-term conditions. Prevention, assessment and treatment of pain management improved. Integrated Children's Community teams and Community Children's nursing services working outside hospital
7. Children and young people in hospital	Children and young people receive high-quality, evidence-based hospital care, developed through clinical governance and delivered in appropriate settings	Care integrated and co-ordinated around their needs. Play for children in hospital is essential. Children, young people and their families treated with respect, involved in decision-making about their care, and given choices. Planned discharge from hospital for children. Hospital stay kept to a minimum. High-quality evidence-based care provided. Hospitals meet responsibilities to safeguard and promote welfare of children. Care is provided in an appropriate location and in a safe environment.

Table 5.5 (*Continued*)

8. **Disabled children and young people and those with complex health needs**	Children and young people who are disabled or who have complex health needs, receive co-ordinated, high-quality child and family-centred services which are based on assessed needs, which promote social inclusion and, where possible, enable them and their families to live ordinary lives.	Services promote social inclusion. Increased access to hospital and primary health care services, therapy and equipment services, and social services. Early identification of health conditions, impairments and physical barriers to inclusion through integrated diagnosis and assessment processes. Early intervention and support to parents. Palliative care is available where needed. Services have robust systems to safeguard disabled children and young people. Multi-agency transition planning occurs to support adulthood.
9. **The mental health and psychological well-being of children and young people**	All children and young people, from birth to their eighteenth birthday, who have mental health problems and disorders have access to timely, integrated, high-quality multi-disciplinary mental health services to ensure effective assessment, treatment and support, for them and their families	Professional support for children's mental health is available in the early years. Staff working with children and young people contribute to early intervention and mental health promotion and develop good partnerships with children. Improved access to CAMHS with high-quality multi-disciplinary CAMHS teams working in a range of settings. Gaps in service addressed particularly for those with learning disabilities. Care Networks developed and care in appropriate and safe settings.
10. **Medicines for children and young people**	Children, young people, their parents or carers, and health care professionals in all settings make decisions about medicines based on sound information about risk and benefit. They have access to safe and effective medicines that are prescribed on the basis of the best available evidence.	Safe medication practice. Use of unlicensed and off-label medicines comply with local and safety standards. Enhanced decision support for prescribers. Improved access to medicines. Clear, understandable, up-to-date information provided on medicines to users and parents. Greater support for those taking medication at home, in care and in education settings – safe storage, supply and administration of medicines. Equitable access to medicines and to safeguard children in special circumstances, disabled children and those with mental health disorders. Pharmacists' expertise is fully utilised.
11. **Maternity services**	Women have easy access to supportive, high-quality maternity services, designed around their individual needs and those of their babies	Women-centred care with easy access to information and support. Care pathways and managed care networks. Improved pre-conception care and access to a midwife as first point of contact. Local perinatal psychiatric services available. Choice of where best to give birth, i.e. home or maternity unit. Post-birth care provided based on a structured assessment. Breast-feeding information and support for mothers

Table 5.6 The division of responsibilities between schools and local authorities for SEN monitoring (Source: DfES 2004b)

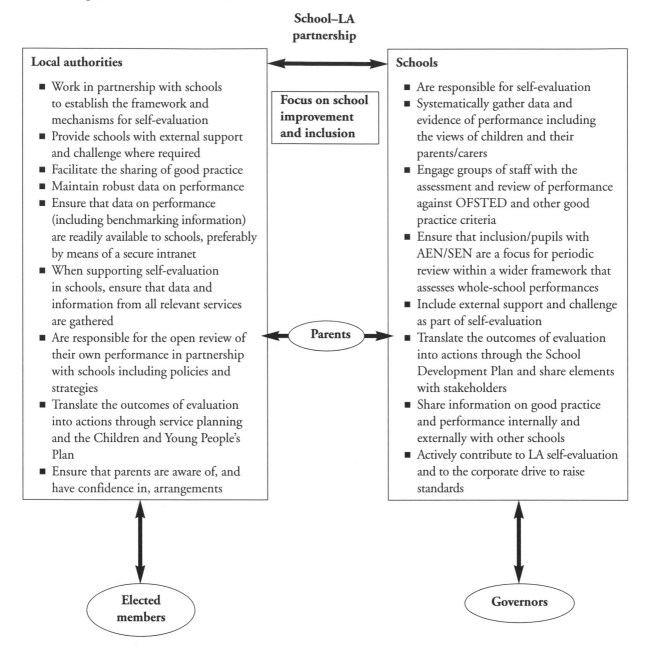

Table 5.7 Example school SEN profile (Source: DfES 2005)

Maple School		**SEN School Profile**

SENCO: Mr Brookes

SEN Governor: Mrs Fish

Description: Maple School is an inclusive extended school for pupils aged 3–11. It is located on the same site as Mason High School, and Slade Special School. It is part of a Networked Learning Community.

SEN Team	SEN Website
School **Admissions Policy**	*Summary of SEN Policy*

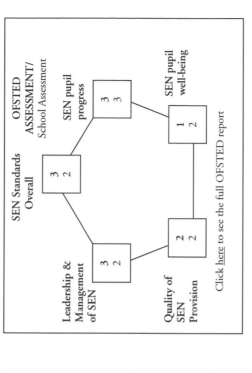

SEN Standards Overall — OFSTED ASSESSMENT/ School Assessment

SEN pupil progress

Leadership & Management of SEN

SEN pupil well-being

Quality of SEN Provision

Click here to see the full OFSTED report

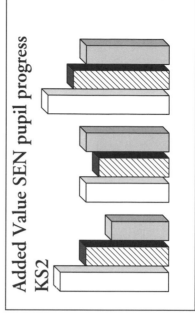

Added Value SEN pupil progress KS2

What is good about SEN in Maple School?

A diversity of pupils with SEN attend this school: those with learning difficulties, sensory impairments, physical disabilities, and behavioural, emotional and social difficulties. SEN pupils are included in all aspects of school life, and are given every opportunity to fulfil their potential. The wellbeing of every child in Maple School matters. The school's Learning Zone caters for the full ability range of pupils, from those with learning difficulties to those who are gifted and talented. The Learning Zone supports personalised learning, enhances and extends learning through access to 'state of the art' ICT, and also offers pupils personalised services, i.e. therapeutic interventions from health and social services. A successful mentoring scheme operates, where older pupils act as 'study buddies' to younger pupils with SEN.

SEN Priorities:

Our four priorities for the year are:
(1) Undertake joint inclusive learning opportunities with staff and pupils from Slade Special School
(2) Introduce smaller stepped assessment, i.e. PIVATS, for SEN pupils
(3) Involve SEN pupils more in reviewing their own progress and SEN provision
(4) Increase the number of laptop computers for SEN pupils to undertake home and distance learning

Curriculum flexibility and access for SEN pupils

All SEN pupils receive their full curriculum entitlement. Personalised learning approaches ensure that pupils are active participants in their learning. Access to ICT is available across the curriculum. Additional support is available in literacy, numeracy, speech and language therapy and pupil counselling to those SEN pupils who require further interventions. This is undertaken in small groups or on an individual basis.

All SEN pupils have access to out-of-hours learning activities, school trips and residential experiences. SEN pupils are represented on the Pupils' Forum.

Click *here* to view some of the out-of-hours learning activities SEN pupils have been involved in.

6

Quality Assurance Role for SENCOs

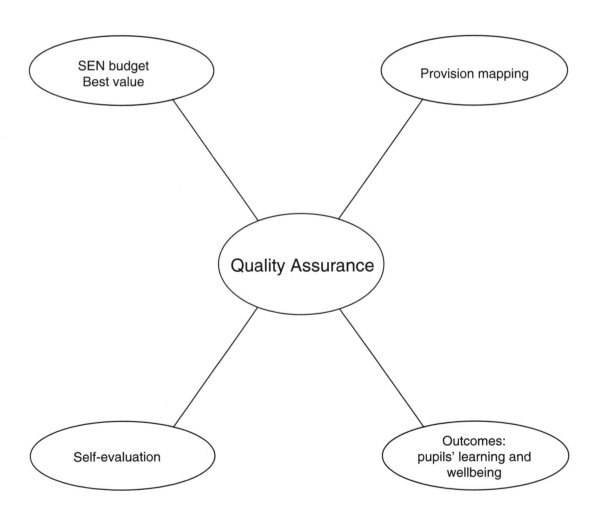

OFSTED, in their HMI report on SEN and disability in mainstream schools, found that:

> Few schools evaluate their provision for pupils with SEN systematically so that they can establish how effective the provision is and whether it represents value for money. (OFSTED 2004a: 5)

This chapter provides SENCOs with practical tools to quality assure SEN provision.

Evidence to include:

- average gains made by children receiving additional help for literacy/numeracy, speech and language inputs, behaviour interventions;
- percentage of children with SEN attaining nationally expected levels for the key stage; and
- progress made by children with below average starting points over key stage (value added point score).
- Complete the school evaluation of impact outcomes of SEN provision record sheet above in early September.
- Attach SEN provision map for that academic year to this sheet, with a copy of the self-evaluation form for accounting for annual SEN budget amounts.
- Send these documents electronically to the named officer at the local authority by the end of September, and also provide a copy to your head teacher and SEN governor.

Table 6.1 SENCO role in managing and monitoring the SEN budget (Source: DfES 2005a)

Focusing	Developing	Establishing	Enhancing
All the available SEN budget is used to provide for the individual needs of children as set out in IEPs and statements	• Needs of SEN pupils are beginning to be analysed more systematically across Year groups or subjects • Resource allocations for SEN are tied more closely to analysis of pupils' needs • The SENCO influences the budget-setting process and manages agreed SEN resources	• Resources are allocated against explicit criteria, published in the school's SEN policy, and against an audit of children's needs • Some monitoring and evaluation of the impact of resources deployed is undertaken • The SENCO and head teacher can demonstrate the impact of resources on children with SEN and the governors are aware of these	• Resources are allocated with maximum efficiency in line with the objectives for SEN and inclusion, as set out in the school development plan • There are well-established systems for monitoring and evaluating the impact of additional provision • Governors, head teacher, SMT and the SENCO collaborate over the budget-setting process and management of resources • Data relating to the needs of individual pupils and groups of children inform the budget-setting process
SEN is clearly identified as a budget heading	• Value for money is taken into account in planning the SEN budget • The school budget contains clear information about allocations to various aspects of SEN	• Value for money is carefully monitored • Detailed SEN expenditure is identified and matched against SEN pupil progress	• All appropriate governors and managers are able to identify value for money in SEN by relating budget headings to data relating to SEN children's progress

SEN provision maps

Provision mapping is a succinct way for schools to show the range of additional and different provision made available to SEN pupils on the graduated response of the SEN Code of Practice.

Table 6.2 Self-evaluation form for accounting for annual SEN budget amounts

		Last financial year (actual) (£)	This financial year (forecast) (£)

Income

A	Notional SEN budget (AWPU)		
B	SEN funding Formula – (FSM, attainment)		
C	Any other income in support of learners with special educational needs not included in (A) or (B) (e.g. EiC, Strategy funding, LMS scheme)		
D	Total income in support of learners with special educational needs		

Expenditure

E	Expenditure through an LEA-designated unit (including in-class and withdrawal support)		
F	Expenditure associated with statements of SEN for individual learners (not included in E)		
G	Any other identifiable expenditure associated with pupils with SEN supported through School Action or Action Plus (not included in E or F)		
H	Total expenditure in support of learners with special educational needs		

School:_____

Table 6.3 School evaluation of impact/outcomes of SEN provision

Year group	No. of SEN pupils in year group at Action, Action Plus and Statement	Evidence of impact/SEN pupil outcomes SEN data analysis findings – FFT, FS Profile, ECM outcomes
Year	Action Action Plus Statement	
Year	Action Action Plus Statement	
Year	Action Action Plus Statement	
Year	Action Action Plus Statement	
Year	Action Action Plus Statement	

They are a comprehensive means of accounting for SEN provision that SEN children have accessed over time. Provision maps who may be for those pupils with relatively common low-level needs Complement Group Education Plans (GEPs) at Action, routinely met through group provision such as Wave 2 literacy or numeracy interventions like ELS, ALS, FLS, as well as IEPs for more complex SEN pupils at Action as well as at Action Plus and Statement. The provision map has to be costed, is maintained annually and, where necessary, particularly where there is a transient SEN pupil population, reviewed and revised termly.

Types of provision map

There are various models for provision maps that can be utilised to record succinctly the SEN provision put in place within a school. There are good examples provided in the National Primary Strategy Materials 2005: *Leading on Inclusion*, and also in the KS3 National Strategy 2005: *Maximising, Progress: Ensuring the Attainment of Pupils with SEN*, and in Gross and White (2003).

Listed below are some of the most popular types of provision maps being used by schools for SEN:

- maps by Wave interventions (Wave 2, Wave 3);
- maps by SEN Code of Practice graduated response threshold (Action, Action Plus and Statement);
- maps by year group or key stage; and
- maps by SEN category – as recorded in the Pupil Level Annual Schools Census (PLASC).

Advantages of provision mapping:

- provides an overview of provision for all SEN pupils in a school to a range of stakeholders, e.g. parents, SEN governor, LA SEN officers, OFSTED inspectors;
- indicates where there may be gaps in SEN provision;
- low maintenance in terms of administration and maintenance, reducing SEN bureaucracy;
- where IEPs are required, information from the provision map can be pasted in electronically to the IEP;
- provides an at-a-glance overview to class and subject teachers of the level of additional provision SEN pupils are receiving, which supports their planning.

Disadvantages of provision mapping

- initially time-consuming to gather information to compile provision map;
- when SEN pupil transience is high, revision of provision maps has to be done more regularly;
- heavily reliant on computer access;
- provision map may not include all necessary information that an IEP would, e.g. targets, strategies to meet targets set, pupil's self-review.

Evaluating and reviewing SEN provision maps

SENCOs would find it helpful to work their way through answering the following questions, in order to better inform SEN provision mapping:

1. What are the data revealing about the impact of each type of provision, and additional intervention?

Table 6.4 Model framework for an SEN provision map (Foundation stage/Primary phase)

YEAR	Additional and different Provision/ resource (Action, Action Plus, Statement/Wave 2, 3 Interventions)	Cost per week (£) Time/ hours, staff/Pupil ratio and who Provides inputs	Total annual cost (£) and source of funding
Nursery			
Reception			
1			
2			
3			
4			
5			
6			

Table 6.5 Model framework for an SEN provision map (Secondary phase)

YEAR	Additional and different Provision/ resource (School Action, School Action Plus, Statement)	Cost per week (£) Time/ hours, staff/Pupil ratio and who Provides inputs	Total annual cost (£) and source of funding
7			
8			
9			
10			
11			
12/13			

2. What are the views of stakeholders, e.g. parents/carers, pupils, staff, governors, external professionals, on the effectiveness of the additional SEN provision made?
3. Are there any provisions in the map, which are no longer viewed as additional?
4. Which have been the most effective interventions for SEN pupils, and how has the evidence of impact been disseminated as good practice to other schools and SENCOs?
5. What modifications will have to be made to the current SEN provision map in order to meet the needs of new SEN pupils joining the school, at the beginning of the academic year?

Value for money

OFSTED noted in their HMI report that:

> SENCOs play no role in financial decision-making and nor do they contribute sufficiently
> to the overall evaluation of provision for pupils with SEN. (OFSTED 2004a: para. 95)

The NUT Survey (2004) on SENCOs and the Revised SEN Code of Practice in relation to SEN
funding and SENCOs, found that:

- greater clarity is required about the SEN budget in schools, particularly in relation to SENCOs knowing the exact amount provided and how to use it appropriately;
- more consensus about what local authority services are available to schools to commission and purchase;
- greater clarity needed as to what provision schools should expect to secure from their delegated SEN budget for particular groups of SEN pupils;
- SENCOs require further training in managing SEN expenditure.

Table 6.6 Evaluating the impact of additional SEN provision on outcomes for SEN pupils

Aspect of SEN provision	Evidence/evaluative judgement, comment
What impact are additional resources, accommodation and additional staffing committed to SEN, having on SEN pupils' progress, attainments, achievement and well-being?	
How are you reviewing the cost-effectiveness of the impact of SEN funding on pupils' attainment, progress, achievement and well-being?	
How are you identifying the budgetary provision to meet the additional needs of SEN pupils?	
How are you using delegated funding effectively to meet the needs of SEN pupils on each threshold of the SEN Code of Practice graduated approach?	
Which are the best features of your additional provision for SEN pupils and why?	
Which aspects of SEN provision require improvement, and what action are you taking?	

Table 6.7 OFSTED criteria for self-evaluation of SEN and inclusion (Source: OFSTED 2004a: 25)

The criteria below contribute to the process of school self-evaluation of the effectiveness of provision for SEN in mainstream schools. They can provide a useful checklist for SENCOs

Progress	Curriculum access
■ At least 80% of pupils make the nationally expected gains of two levels at KS2 and one level at KS3 ■ 78% of pupils who begin KS2 at level 1 in English achieve level 3 by the end of KS2 ■ At least 34% of pupils below level 2 in English in Year 7 make a one-level gain by the end of KS3 and 55% of pupils at level 2 make this gain ■ Pupils withdrawn for substantial literacy support make an average of double the normal rate of progress ■ The attendance of pupils with special needs is good (above 92%) and unauthorised absence is low	■ Sensitive allocation to teaching groups and careful modification of the curriculum, timetables and social arrangements is made ■ The pupils whose reading ages fall below their peers have access to special help ■ The curriculum is reviewed annually in the light of a regular audit of pupils' needs and the school responds to the outcomes of the review by establishing additional and/or different programmes of study to meet their needs ■ Plans to innovate are included in the school disability access plan ■ Partnership between mainstream and special schools focuses on the development of the curriculum and teaching and enhances the opportunities available for pupils in both mainstream and special schools
Teaching and learning	**Wellbeing**
■ There is widespread awareness among staff of the particular needs of pupils and understanding of the practical ways of meeting those needs in classrooms ■ Assessment is regular and thorough and is used to plan future work and help pupils understand how they can improve ■ Teachers have high expectations of what can be achieved and set challenging targets ■ Lessons use appropriate methods to ensure pupils learn and enjoy their work ■ Suitable resources including ICT are available to enable access to the curriculum	■ There is an active approach to personal and social development, as well as to learning, in the school, especially to lessen the effects of the divergence of social interests between older pupils with SEN and their peers ■ All pupils learn about disability issues ■ Pupils with SEN have a 'voice' in the school which is heard regularly ■ Pupils with SEN and disability are able to participate fully in the life of the school ■ There are well-defined and consistently applied approaches to managing difficult behaviour

Inclusion policy and practice
■ Admissions and exclusions are monitored and analysed (in relation to placements in other schools) ■ Pupils with disabilities whose parents request a place at the school are admitted wherever possible and the school makes reasonable adjustments to include them in the life of the school ■ There is careful preparation of placements, covering the pupils with SEN, their peers in school, parents and staff, with careful attention to the availability of sufficient suitable teaching and personal support ■ Trends over time in National Curriculum and other assessments are analysed in the context of available data about comparative performance and are scrutinised ■ Pupils' work is regularly discussed and the quality of teaching of pupils with SEN is regularly observed ■ Evaluation of the quality of provision is linked to the information about the outcomes for pupils ■ Those responsible are held to account for the quality of the provision, and plans to improve the outcomes are implemented ■ The school integrates its systems and procedures for pupils with SEN (including arrangements for assessment, recording and reporting) into the overall arrangements for all pupils ■ Deliberate steps are taken to involve parents of pupils with SEN as fully as possible in decision-making, keeping them well informed about their child's progress and giving them as much practical support as possible

Table 6.8 SEN monitoring and evaluation cycle for schools (Academic year: September to July)

Term	Monitoring focus	Methods of monitoring	Responsibility for monitoring
Autumn 1 (July–October)	**SEN pupil progress/achievement reviewed** (prior attainment)	Data analysis (FS Profile, NC levels, P-scales/PIVATS, EBD scales, attendance, exclusions)	Head teacher, Assessment Co-ordinator, Subject Leaders
		Baseline assessment undertaken	SENCO
		Findings from last IEP/IBP, statement review	SENCO
		Annual Report to Parents on SEN	SENCO/Head teacher/SEN Governor
	Planning and implementation of SEN provision, Wave interventions, catch-up programmes, SEN programmes for pupils at Action, Action+, Statement	SEN Provision map formulated, linked to SEN funding/additional resources	SENCO
		New IEPs/IBPs put in place (SENCO time with relevant staff)	SENCO with class/subject teachers, pastoral leaders
		SEN Register updated	Administrative support for SENCO
	Staff SEN/Inclusion CPD needs identified	Staff CPD audit for SEN/Inclusion	SENCO
Autumn 2 (November–December)	**Monitoring of SEN pupil progress and of SEN provision** (quality first teaching, intervention programmes, curriculum differentiation, access)	IEPs/IBPs, statements reviewed and revised	SENCO, class/subject teachers, pastoral staff
		Focused lesson observations (paired)	SENCO with Head/Deputy, Subject leader
		Scrutiny of teacher planning	SENCO
		Sampling of SEN pupils' work across the curriculum	SENCO
		Discussions about pupil progress and SEN provision with teachers, TAs, pupil, parents, external professionals	SENCO
		SEN INSET/CPD for staff (to support and advise on curriculum differentiation, access and delivery, behaviour management)	SENCO and/or external professional
		Meeting with SEN Governor to report on progress and monitor SEN provision	SENCO/SEN governor
Spring 1 (January–February)	**Monitoring, review and evaluation of interim progress of SEN pupils following catch-up, Wave 3 or SEN intervention programmes**	Data analysis of pupil attainment (learning and/or behaviour)	SENCO, Assessment co-ordinator, Literacy and numeracy co-ordinator, pastoral leader
		Re-assessment of SEN pupils, as appropriate	SENCO
		Scrutiny of pupils' work in programmes	SENCO
		Discussion with staff, pupil, parents, external professionals about pupil progress, provision.	SENCO
		SEN Register updated	Administrative support for SENCO

Table 6.8 (*Continued*)

Spring 1 (January–February)	Reassessment of SEN pupils requiring exam concessions, additional support	SENCO, external professionals (as appropriate) Assessment co-ordinator/SENCO
	Identification of SEN pupils requiring exam concessions and support, and application made to QCA	
Spring 2 (February–March/April)	Pupil progress (Y6), reviewed and statement advice and provision revised, updated	SENCO, external professionals
	Transition reviews completed for pupils with statements of SEN	
	Focused SEN monitoring (e.g. use of ICT across the curriculum, access, behaviour management)	
	Lesson observation and sampling pupils work/achievements	SENCO, head teacher, deputy head, subject leader
	Review and revision of IEPs/IBPs, statements	SENCO, class/subject teachers, pastoral staff
	Discussion with staff, pupil, parents, external professionals	SENCO
	SEN Register updated	Administrative support for SENCO
Summer 1 (April–May)	Moderation of teacher assessment (P-scales, PIVATS, FS Profile. NC levels, EBD scale) by standardising samples of work for SEN pupils	SENCO, subject co-ordinator, assessment co-ordinator, external consultant (as appropriate)
	Monitoring of assessment for learning for SEN pupils	
	Forward planning for SEN budget	
	Bids/proposals submitted for SEN linked to priorities on SDP, national priorities, SEN development plan	SENCO, head teacher, curriculum co-ordinator
Summer 2 (June–July)	Taster days, pupil support sessions, exchange of information, data between settings, meeting with parents	SENCO, deputy head
	Transition preparation	
	Review of SEN pupil progress and achievement	
	Data collection, analysis (teacher assessment)	SENCO
	End of year assessment (standardised tests for reading, spelling, numeracy)	SENCO
	Scrutiny of pupils' work with n specific intervention programmes, and across the curriculum	SENCO
	Lesson observations	SENCO, head teacher, deputy head teacher
	Discussions with staff, pupil, parents/carers	SENCO
	Planning and review meeting with external professionals about pupil progress, future case work involvement	SENCO
	Review of IEPs/IBPs, statements	SENCO, class/subject teachers, TAs, pastoral staff
	SEN Register reviewed and updated	Administrative support for SENCO

(*Continued*)

Table 6.8 (*Continued*)

Term	Monitoring focus	Methods of monitoring	Responsibility for monitoring
Summer 2 (June–July)	**SEN budget review** (end of academic year)	Scrutiny of SEN budget expenditure	SENCO, Bursar, head teacher
		Evaluation of SEN provision map	SENCO
		Meeting with the SEN governor to report on SEN provision and pupil progress (value added)	SENCO, SEN governor
	End of year evaluation of SEN policy and provision (impact and effectiveness of additional interventions/provision – value-added progress)	Completion of ongoing self-evaluation framework for monitoring and evaluating SEN policy and provision	SENCO, head teacher
		Meeting with SEN governor to report on SEN pupil progress and impact of additional SEN provision/interventions, initiatives, developments, access plan targets	SENCO, SEN governor
		Updating SEN policy	SENCO
	SEN development plan review and revision	Using outcomes from school self-review of SEN policy and provision; survey findings from stakeholders (pupils, parents, staff, external professionals).	SENCO

Table 6.9 School self-evaluation framework for SEN provision and *Every Child Matters* outcomes for children and young people

Criteria for judging the quality of SEN policy and provision – whole school. The scores correspond to OFSTED's judgement criteria.

1	2	3	4
Outstanding	**Good**	**Satisfactory**	**Inadequate**
Highly inclusive; pupils with SEN enjoy their education; highly effective teaching; very good progress in meeting challenging targets set for SEN; standards moving up rapidly; effective quality assurance procedures; SEN provision very good value for money; school's SEN and inclusion very well regarded by parents and wider community; very good improvement in SEN since last inspection	Inclusion central to work of the school; very few SEN pupils under-perform; teaching is effective; curriculum meets needs very well; good progress made towards meeting targets set for SEN; SEN pupils relate well to peers and respect other staff; SEN pupils are keen to learn and behave well; Good care and guidance is provided to SEN pupils; parents have confidence in school's SEN provision; good improvement in SEN since last inspection	Targets for SEN whole school are reasonably challenging; most pupils with SEN enjoy school and make satisfactory progress in learning and personal development; small pockets of disaffection exist; a little under-performance among SEN pupils; areas of teaching and curriculum for SEN pupils need improvement; steady progress made to improve; resources for SEN are adequate; satisfactory value for money	Targets for SEN whole school are not met and are not challenging; many pupils with SEN do not enjoy their education; SEN pupils don't make adequate progress; SEN pupil disaffection is high; significant weaknesses in teaching and the curriculum; health and safety of SEN pupils is at risk; wellbeing is inadequately promoted for pupils with SEN; leadership and management of SEN lacks direction; pupil performance is not evaluated accurately; SEN provision gives unsatisfactory value for money and is held in low regard by parents and the community

Annual school self-review of SEN policy and provision, as part of the new relationship with schools process, helps to evaluate the impact that additional SEN provision, Wave 3 and Wave 2 catch-up interventions have on SEN pupils' outcomes in relation to their inclusion, achievements, attainment, progress, personal development and wellbeing.

Through the process of school self-evaluation, head teachers and SENCOs with the SEN governor will confirm that the school clearly knows the needs of the pupils with SEN, what they are achieving, the quality of the teaching they receive, whether the curriculum is matched to their needs, how well they are supported and how effectively provision is monitored and evaluated.

The entire framework can be used if the school has not had an OFSTED inspection for some years. Aspects of SEN policy and provision may be focused on if the school undertakes a regular annual review of SEN whole school, which addresses SDP priorities.

The school self-evaluation SEN framework aligns with the revised OFSTED inspection schedule and with the five outcomes for the wellbeing of children and young people, as set out in *Every Child Matters* and the Children Act 2004. These are:

1. *Being healthy* – **physically, mentally and emotionally healthy; making healthy choices and having a healthy lifestyle.**
   Pupils with SEN and disabilities undertake PE, sport; pupils drink water at regular intervals; eat healthily; recognise and manage stress. Staff are supported in identifying possible physical and mental problems related to SEN pupils and make appropriate referrals. Pupils have access to a range of support if troubled.

Table 6.9 (*Continued*)

2. *Staying safe* – safe from bullying and discrimination; safe from crime and anti-social behaviour in and out of school; safe from neglect, violence, maltreatment, accidental injury, sexual exploitation. Pupils have security, stability and are cared for.

   Contingency plans for disaster in place; fire drills take place; staff are trained to identify risks and manage them; staff are CRB checked; there is a designated member of staff for child protection who receives regular training; staff responsible for child protection are well supported and supervised; clear threshold criteria for referral and responding to child protection issues are clear and widely understood. Pupils are taught to swim.

3. *Enjoying and achieving* – ready for school; attend and enjoy school; achieve personal and social development and enjoy recreation; achieve and make good progress in relation to their starting points throughout their schooling; pupils have their learning supported by their parents/carers, family.

   Support is given to pupils with poor behaviour and attendance; pupils' personal and academic development is monitored and appropriate provision to meet pupils' needs is in place; development planning targets the needs of potentially underachieving groups, e.g. SEN, vulnerable children, children in public care.

4. *Make a positive contribution to the community* – develop positive relationships and do not bully or discriminate; develop self-confidence and deal successfully with life changes and challenges; engage in law-abiding, positive behaviour; engage in decision-making and support the community and environment.

   SEN pupils know their rights and responsibilities; SEN pupils are free from bullying and discrimination; SEN pupils initiate and manage a range of organised activities; SEN pupils are consulted about key decisions that affect them and their views are listened to; pupils learn how to become responsible citizens; clear school policies on combating bullying and discrimination are in place. SEN pupils who are victims of bullying and harassment know how to raise concerns and are given good access to support.

5. *Enjoying social and economic wellbeing* – live in decent homes and sustainable communities; have access to transport and material goods; engage in further education, employment or training on leaving school; are ready for employment.

   SEN pupils are supported in developing self-confidence, team working skills and enterprising qualities; impartial careers advice is available and personal support is provided for SEN pupils; work-based learning and work experience is provided in KS4. SEN pupils are financially literate.

The purpose of this school self-evaluation SEN framework is to enable the head teacher and SENCO, in partnership with external professionals, to judge the quality of SEN policy and provision, matched against the OFSTED grading criteria and the *Every Child Matters* five outcomes for children and young people. It will enable schools to evaluate their provision for pupils with SEN more systematically, establish how effective the additional provision is, whether it represents value for money, and how it leads to improving standards of achievement for pupils with SEN.

The full self-evaluation framework can be downloaded from the CD accompanying this book.

7

Reducing Bureaucracy

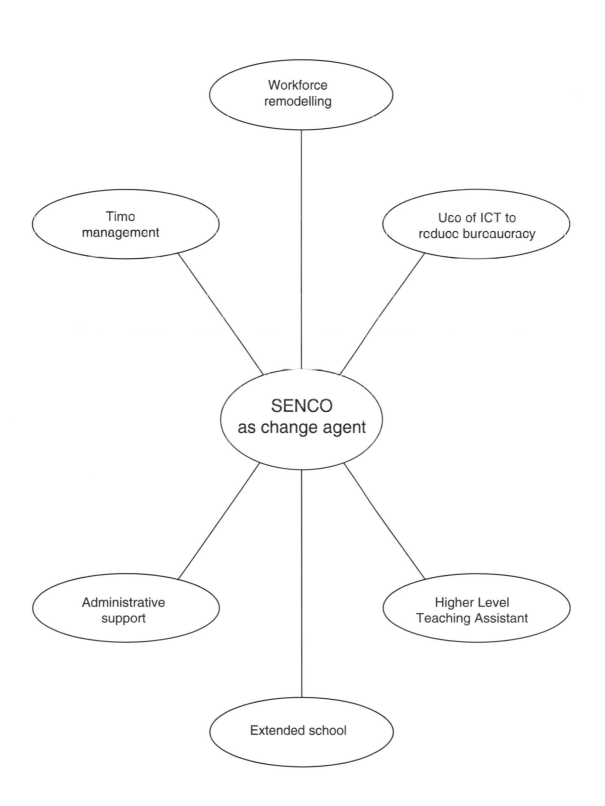

The national perspective on SEN bureaucracy

The DfES Circular 2/98, Reducing the Bureaucratic Burden on Teachers, comments on SEN:

> The Secretary of State looks to LEAs, headteachers and teachers to work together to ensure that effective action is taken in this field, and that unjustified demands for information are not made.

The SEN Code of Practice (DfES 2001b), also recommended that the SENCO should:

- keep records of the steps taken to meet the needs of individual children with special educational needs;
- maintain appropriate individual and whole-school records of children at Action, Action Plus and those with statements;
- oversee the records of all children with special educational needs.

The Code goes on to indicate that: 'The role of the SENCO is time consuming and therefore it is usually inappropriate for the SENCO to have other school-wide responsibilities'. It further adds:

> In many schools the governing body has been able to allocate some administrative staff time to help the SENCO, thus releasing the SENCO to use their expertise more effectively.

> Headteachers and governors should support the SENCO in the use of ICT for SEN management systems and for preparing and recording IEPs. (DfES 2001b: 5.24, 5.33–5.36)

The government, in *Removing Barriers to Achievement*, identified concerns about SEN bureaucracy and outlined the next steps for tackling and reducing this bureaucracy.

> There are significant concerns about the volume of 'bureaucracy' related to the statutory framework on SEN. We take these concerns very seriously, not least because we know that this is diverting skilled staff from spending more time in the classroom. Some procedures and paperwork may be unavoidable as a result of statutory requirements. But the procedures can be operated in an inefficient or unhelpful way . . . Reducing administrative burdens on SENCOs and specialist local authority staff will free up capacity for them to spend more time working directly with pupils and teachers. (DfES 2004a: 1.21)

The DfES outlined the four issues it wanted to tackle in relation to reducing SEN bureaucracy in its *Strategy for SEN* (RBA). These were as follows:

- annual reviews – identifying and promoting effective streamlined procedures;
- IEPs – there is no statutory requirement for schools to prepare separate IEPs for all pupils with SEN as long as they have sound arrangements for monitoring their progress in conjunction with the child and their parents (provision maps are recommended as an alternative to IEPs by the DfES);
- record keeping – identifying effective ICT solutions to manage and handle SEN-related paperwork;
- duplication of data held by different professionals – saving time and using resources more effectively by developing protocols for enabling professional staff working with the same child to have access to the same records wherever possible and work within a common framework. (DfES 2004a: 1.23)

Recommendations for reducing SEN bureaucracy

The DfES Special Educational Needs and Disability Division (SEND) and the Cabinet Office's Regulatory Impact Unit's Public Sector Team (PST) collaborated on a project to identify and recommend practical measures to reduce bureaucracy and paperwork associated with SEN processes.

Thirty-four recommendations for future action were made which focused on three aspects of SEN bureaucracy:

- removing duplication and streamlining processes by which LAs request updated SEN information from schools;
- facilitating information sharing and closer working, i.e. providing clear guidance on data protection, confidentiality and sharing of information between partner agencies;
- providing clarity of roles and expectations, i.e. ensuring all SEN funding is clear and transparent for schools requiring minimal paper-based evidence for its allocation; and providing guidance and training to school governors and senior managers on effective monitoring and clear, specific reporting of SEN outcomes to parents.

The recommendations made in the report were consistent and compatible with the fast-moving changes brought about by *Every Child Matters* and the Children Act 2004. Implementation timescales for the recommended actions were:

- short-term – 12 months
- medium-term – one to two years
- long-term – five years or longer.

The overall benefit of the recommended actions will enable frontline staff in schools and LA children's services to spend more time and energy on meeting effectively the needs of children with SEN, rather than on unnecessary bureaucratic procedures and systems.

Reducing and cutting the burdens of bureaucracy for SENCOs

Cutting bureaucracy is a key element of successful remodelling to allow schools to concentrate on the essentials of teaching and learning, and the wellbeing of children and young people.

The first, and most straightforward, strategy for reducing bureaucracy for SENCOs is simply to stop doing things that do not have a direct impact on pupils' learning and wellbeing. This is referred to as cost–benefit analysis, where SENCOs review, judge and decide if there would be any benefit in doing non-essential bureaucratic tasks.

Examples of when SENCOs can reasonably stop doing a bureaucratic activity relate largely to the collection or analysis of information, for example when:

- the output(s) of the activity is no longer needed;
- a new information request has been introduced which wholly or partly supersedes an earlier request;
- you are being asked to summarise information already supplied, possibly in a different format or already in the public domain;
- the information, while claimed to be needed, is not as, far as you can see, acted upon, i.e. it makes no discernible difference to the learning of SEN pupils in your care;
- the information-collection activity is carried out more often than the information is required; or
- the information has been prepared purely for the benefit of a third party.

In all the above instances you are entitled, as SENCO, to raise the issue of whether you need to supply the information requested, and to assess what justification is given for the information request. The SENCO should make contact with whoever requested the information, and ask them to justify it. This management strategy relates only to any information not required by law,

Table 7.1 Summary of recommendations related to reducing SEN bureaucracy (Source: DfES/Cabinet office RIU 2004: 5–7, 11–12)

Action	Timescale
Record keeping – IEPs and other plans	
DfES to: ■ Review the use of the different plans for children with the aim of consolidating and integrating into a single child plan	**Short Term** (12 months)
Inter-agency working and information sharing	
LAs and schools to: ■ Make greater use of information from their own administrative databases in order to pre-populate forms with basic information held on the child	**Short Term** (12 months)
Paperwork	
LAs and other statutory service providers to: ■ Minimise the demand for information regarding individual children already held on their own systems, by only making requests for updated information or assessments	**Short Term** (12 months)
SENCO role	
DfES to: ■ Establish and provide guidance on criteria and sources of funding for the provision of non-contact time and administrative support for the SENCO as part of Phase 3 of the Workforce Agreement ■ Disseminate effective models of SEN co-ordination	**Medium Term** (1 to 2 years)
School governing bodies to: ■ Consider the role of the SENCO and the input of additional demands and new initiatives on the SENCO's ability to carry out the role effectively ■ Provide training and professional development opportunities for all teachers on meeting special educational needs	**Medium Term** (1 to 2 years)
Benefits	
Efforts to reduce bureaucracy and red tape will only go some way to relieving the burden on SENCOs and needs to be accompanied by a clearer consideration of the roles and responsibilities of all staff who work with children and young people experiencing difficulties in learning. A clear indication of SENCOs' responsibilities and effective use of release time will enable SENCOs to fulfil their role effectively and enable colleagues to understand the parameters of the role. This would also facilitate an improved SEN service.	
Other actions taken would review and provide clarification of the responsibilities of different parties in making provision for special educational needs. They would enable efficient monitoring and the sharing of good practice in minimising bureaucracy and review effectiveness and, best value of all, the actions taken in relation to the statutory framework. They would demonstrate that full account is being taken of the views expressed and issues raised by stakeholders in relation to meeting the needs of children with special educational needs within the current statutory framework.	

where the SENCO does not have a legal duty. However, currently, much of this information is a legal requisite under the SEN Code of Practice, in relation to pupils with statements of special educational needs. Reducing the number of statements issued may therefore help to alleviate the extensiveness of the SEN bureaucracy (paperwork) required.

In any review of workload through cost–benefit task analysis and mapping of activities cross-role, SENCOs must be assured that the reduction in SEN bureaucracy enables them to carry out their role more efficiently (doing things right), as well as effectively (doing the right things), and that successful SEN management will foster success in others, within the school's SEN and Inclusion Team.

The SENCO will interface regularly with the governing body and, in particular, the SEN governor, in order to provide SEN information to enable them to fulfil their statutory responsibilities. Clearly, the DfES views the governing body as being influential in, and supportive of, special education, and in facilitating and supporting a manageable workload for the SENCO in the school.

The Chief HMI, in his annual report 2003/2004, commented:

> . . . the responsibilities of special educational needs coordinators, in particular, entail a high clerical workload and few had support staff to whom they could delegate this to allow them to concentrate on their leadership role. (OFSTED 2005b: 48.14)

An NUT survey (2004) on SENCOs and the Revised SEN Code of Practice confirmed the Chief HMI's findings:

* considerable administration increase relating to IEPs and the gathering of evidence and the paperwork required for reviews;
* little, if any, time in the school day for SEN paperwork to be done, resulting in many SENCOs completing this outside school hours, at home during evenings, over the weekend or during holiday time;
* difficulty in keeping up with, and on top of, the SEN paperwork, which has increased SENCO workload considerably in inclusive schools;
* provision and access to ICT, in particular the SENCO having a laptop computer. While this makes the administration of SEN more manageable electronically, it does not prevent such work spilling over into home life, and affecting the work/life balance of SENCOs.

One SENCO from the NUT survey remarked:

> School doesn't recognise the amount of work involved with SEN. Lack of non-contact time means several SEN meetings a week after school. No administrative support given as suggested in the new Code. School now inclusive – several pupils with severe disabilities – in principle good but has led to a huge increase in workload. (NUT 2004: 29)

Workforce remodelling

Remodelling increases the capacity to manage future change more effectively. A healthy culture for remodelling and re-conceptualising roles of a school's workforce are reliant on five key factors:

* all staff take responsibility;
* everyone's unique skill is valued;
* staff from all roles are included in problem-solving;
* support staff add value to pupils' learning and wellbeing;
* staff coach and mentor each other in a supportive way, at all levels.

Remodelling supports capacity building in schools, in order to give a better focus on teaching and learning and raising standards:

Teaching and learning	Standards
Planning and preparation	*Every Child Matters* five outcomes
Lesson observation and reflective practice	Improved attendance and behaviour
Personalised learning	Pupil attainment, progress, results
Assessment for learning	Improved motivation in pupils and staff
ICT across the curriculum in classrooms	Improved staff retention and recruitment
CPD for all staff	School more popular in community
Performance management and feedback for all staff	Stakeholders' expectations better met

PriceWaterhouseCoopers' report on teacher workload in 2001 found that, on average, teachers were spending 20 per cent of their time on 25 administrative and supervisory tasks that could be done by others, i.e. support/administrative staff, or reduced by efficient use of ICT.

The ensuing National Agreement has not been about replacing teachers with teaching assistants but about identifying ways in which the support staff roles can be extended in order to free teachers from the shackles of excessive and inappropriate routine administrative and clerical tasks which, in turn, will help to further raise standards in schools.

Remodelling provides school managers, particularly of extended schools, with the opportunity to review their school workforce and to fit differently competent people to different jobs. Auditing the needs of their pupils and the skills of their staff and fitting these together will enable school managers to have a more flexible and varied workforce that will be able to respond more appropriately to the needs of a lifelong learning community, and an organisation that provides a range of services for children and families, in addition to education.

Table 7.2 PriceWaterhouseCoopers' report on teacher workload

Workforce Agreement Phase	Changes implemented
Phase 1 (2003)	■ teachers, including head teachers, not to routinely undertake 24 of the 25 administrative and clerical tasks
	■ teachers, including head teachers, to have a reasonable allocation of time in support of their leadership and management responsibilities
	■ teachers and head teachers to have a reasonable work/life balance
Phase 2 (2004)	■ teachers and head teachers to have a reduced burden of providing cover for absent colleagues. A limit of 38 hours per year, with a view to further reductions
Phase 3 (2005)	■ teachers to have guaranteed planning, preparation and assessment (PPA) time, equivalent to 10% of a teacher's normal timetabled teaching time.
	■ Introduce new arrangements which mean that teachers are not required to invigilate external examinations

SENCOs will have a key role to play in workforce remodelling at school level. They should be on the school's Change Team in order to ensure that the enormity of their role is represented and fully understood in the context of the future challenges presented by *Every Child Matters* and the Strategy for SEN.

The purpose of the Change Team is to:

- share workload issues and views;
- prioritise change initiatives within the school;
- make positive contributions to problem-solving in order to identify workforce solutions;
- act as a communication channel to the whole-school workforce; and
- oversee and implement change initiatives.

Outcomes from Change Team working have meant that some schools have created posts such as Learning Manager, Teaching and Learning Co-ordinator and Key Stage Learning Leaders, explicitly focusing on learning and devising learning pathways aimed at meeting the needs of a diversity of learners.

Vision for the future and remodelling – implications for SENCOs

- fewer highly trained teachers, dealing with larger classes and supported by a range of para-professionals;
- a massively enlarged, well-trained and specialist para-professional workforce supporting small-group work, project work, and carrying out individual pupil mentoring;
- highest paid teachers working for many different schools within a cluster, along with a team of highly qualified para-professionals providing personal tuition and supporting the emotional and social development of individual children;
- new learning professionals, e.g. Excellent teachers for SEN, Leading Teachers in SEN, ASTs for SEN, and the SENCO acting as an SEN/Inclusion Professor or 'virtual' SENCO, employed within a network of schools to teach or act as consultant and adviser, on varied contracts, according to skills;
- less reliance on teachers as learning takes place 'beyond' the classroom;
- teachers and SENCOs leading their own professional development, building unique professional portfolios;
- 'Learning Schools'/Specialist schools in Inclusion and SEN, characterised by flat hierarchies, in which loose teams and networks of diverse expertise often replace formal hierarchies. Quality norms replace regulatory and vertical accountability. Self-evaluation is the norm and, as part of local collaborative arrangements, groups of schools meet regularly and offer their work to others for scrutiny.

Higher level teaching assistants and the SENCO role

DfES Guidance for Schools on Higher Level Teaching Assistant Roles for School Support Staff states:

Teachers and higher level teaching assistants (HLTAs)/support staff are not interchangeable. Accountability for the overall learning outcomes must rest with the teacher. (DfES 2004h: 3)

School support staff, when undertaking specified work, must be subject to the direction and supervision of a teacher in accordance with arrangements made by the headteacher of the school. The headteacher must be satisfied that support staff have the skills, expertise and experience to carry out a range of activities at different levels – including, for some staff, working with whole classes. (ibid.: 4)

Higher level teaching assistant roles have greater complexity and autonomy than other classroom support roles. HLTAs may undertake the more demanding elements of 'specified work' under the direction and supervision of a teacher. This may involve working with individual pupils as well as with groups and whole classes. HLTAs may have other roles involving managing and working with others – for example, guiding the work of other adults (TAs) supporting teaching and learning in the classroom, working collaboratively with colleagues and liaising sensitively and effectively with parents and carers. HLTAs may have multiple roles . . . cover supervision is not an HLTA role . . . and is not an appropriate use of their skills, knowledge and expertise. (DfES 2004h: 11, 14)

The HLTA qualifying National Standards require teaching assistants to demonstrate that they have the knowledge and understanding to help pupils progress. They also cover professional values and practice, and teaching and learning activities such as working with individuals, small groups and in whole-class settings under the direction of a teacher. Skills in planning, monitoring, assessment and class management must also be demonstrated.

Higher level teaching assistants require line management, usually from the SENCO or a deputy head teacher; they are entitled to a formal annual appraisal and continuing professional development. HLTAs are likely to manage, coach, mentor and train other TAs; represent TAs' views at appropriate meetings, and liaise between managers (SENCOs), teaching staff and TAs.

Teaching assistants must meet the TTA national professional standards by undertaking the HLTA assessment and training programme, in order to achieve HLTA status.

There are two routes to obtaining HLTA status:

- by assessment only; or
- through full training.

The assessment-only route is suitable for those teaching assistants who consider that they are already close to the HLTA Standards because of their school experience or training. They must already have a qualification in English and mathematics. The assessment process comprises three days of training and a briefing on the National HLTA Standards, followed by a half-day visit to the assistant's school by an external assessor. The assessor will meet with the head teacher and a teacher who works regularly with the TA.

Full training for HLTAs began in September 2004 and by 2006–7 it is expected that 20,000 TAs will have been trained to become HLTAs in England. This route is designed for TAs who have the potential to become HLTAs, but who require more training. Of the 50 days' training, 20 will take place away from the school. The training will also be supported by school-based activities and on-line support. TAs who undertake HLTA training will need to have obtained an English and mathematics qualification by the end of the training period, if they have not already got these.

Training and assessment is only open to those TAs already working in schools. For some HLTAs, this status is a step on the way to becoming a qualified teacher.

HLTAs should not undertake excessive administrative roles. Like SENCOs, they are not clerical assistants, and too much of this role takes them away from direct work with pupils and parents/carers, where they can have a significant impact.

There is some controversy about whether HLTAs should become SENCOs, and concerns expressed at devaluing the role of the SENCO as a qualified teacher.

The TTA clearly states, in the National Standards for SENCOs, that: 'SENCOs will be skilled teachers in their own subject or phase' (TTA 1998: 9).

A minority of local authorities are providing training to enable HLTAs to become Assistant SENCOs. However, they do not undertake the whole-school strategic leadership and management role for SEN, which is becoming increasingly more challenging as a result of the government's *Every Child Matters: Change for Children* programme. HLTAs may be precluded from higher-level decision-making meetings in a school.

The TTA emphasises that anyone who takes on the SENCO role, such as an HLTA, although they do not need to be a qualified teacher, would have to meet the standard required, in terms of experience and skills. HLTAs may not necessarily have the experience to handle the range of varied and complex queries that are likely to arise from greater multi-agency service working within extended schools and children's centres.

HLTAs need to work under the supervision of a senior teacher, e.g. deputy head teacher, INCO or SENCO, and not work independently. The OFSTED revised inspection framework (September 2005) will be exploring, under the aspect of leadership and management, the capacity of an HLTA to undertake the SENCO role effectively.

Workforce remodelling does offer school managers the opportunity to expand the roles of particular members of the non-teaching staff, which includes HLTAs. In a few instances, an HLTA may be a former qualified teacher with a degree, and with considerable experience of working within a learning support team or department. The head teacher, in such a situation, would need to ensure that the individual meets the HLTA professional standards.

The education profession has been very precious, historically, about teacher status. The SENCO role, in the context of extended schools and *Every Child Matters*, demands many other skills besides teaching. The ideal approach to adopt is a team situation, where learning support staff, which includes HLTA and SENCO, fulfil aspects of the SENCO role that best fit their skills, experience and qualifications, and which earn them credibility and respect within the school.

Schools may establish an *Every Child Matters* Inclusion Team, whereby key staff, including the SENCO, each take responsibility for one of the ECM outcomes, i.e. Child Protection Teacher, PSHE Co-ordinator, Pastoral Deputy Head, Key Stage Co-ordinator.

Time management and the SENCO role

A recommendation was made that one hour per child on the SEN register should be a benchmark measure for SENCO non-contact time. However, there is a lack of clarity as to whether this is one hour per week, per half term, per term or over a year.

The question also has to be asked about whether more non-contact time for the SENCO leads to better results and raised standards for SEN pupils. This is one of the key contextual factors that needs to be taken into account when monitoring and evaluating value-added progress in SEN, at school level. SENCOs may actually receive sufficient non-contact time, but possibly do not utilise this time efficiently, because they devote too much time to SEN paperwork.

Lack of sufficient non-contact time for SENCOs is a major obstacle in enabling them to undertake their role and responsibilities effectively. The SENCO role continues to grow out of all proportion. Government initiatives (national strategies) designed to improve educational standards all require that the SENCO takes on additional work, but do not specify how the time will be found.

The amount of support and time available to SENCOs during the school day has not kept pace with the increased workload and expanding role of the SENCO. The wide variation between schools in the amount of non-contact time allocated to SENCOs is governed by the size of the school, the number of SEN pupils at Action, Action Plus and statement in the school, and any other additional posts of responsibility held by the SENCO.

The SEN Code of Practice made the following recommendations in relation to the time for SEN co-ordination:

- SENCOs require time for:
- planning and co-ordination away from the classroom;
- maintaining appropriate individual and whole-school records of children at Action and Action Plus and those with statements; teaching pupils with SEN;
- observing pupils in class without a teaching commitment;
- managing, supporting and training teaching assistants;
- liaising with colleagues, with early education settings, feeder primary schools and secondary schools, and working with the Connexions Personal Adviser.

(DfES 2001b: 5.33)

The NUT survey on SENCOs and the revised SEN Code of Practice (2004) identified the most usual amounts of specified non-contact time allocated to SENCOs, within the timetabled teaching week to include:

- between one and five hours;
- between six and ten hours;
- between ten and fifteen hours.

Naturally, SENCOs derive the greatest benefit from non-contact time that is allocated in an uninterrupted block of time, such as a whole morning or afternoon. Within a large secondary school, including a higher number of SEN pupils with diverse and more complex and severe needs, two staff are likely to share the SENCO role.

Table 7.3 Exemplar of time allocation for aspects of the SENCO role in mainstream schools

SENCO role activity	Primary (% per year)	Secondary (% per year)
Class, subject teaching, Wave interventions	50	20
Supporting, advising staff, team teaching	18	20
Staff INSET, coaching, mentoring; SENCO CPD	4	6
Administration (with ICT and/or clerical support)	4	5
Meetings with staff, head teacher, governor for SEN	4	9
Liaising and meeting with parents/carers	4	9
Liaising and meeting with external professionals	4	8
Tracking, monitoring pupil progress	3	6
Monitoring, evaluating and reviewing the quality, impact and effectiveness of additional SEN provision	5	8
Time for SEN budget planning, SEN provision mapping and reflection	2	2
Dealing with the unexpected	2	2

Costing SENCO time

The DfES, in relation to the management of SEN expenditure (2004), recommended that local authorities identify an amount within the per pupil allocation to support the cost of SENCO duties and responsibilities:

> The SEN Code of Practice sets out schools' responsibilities including the functions to be undertaken by the SENCO. It makes clear that the cost of SENCO time should come from the school's base budget and not from the additional resources allocated for AEN and SEN. Some LEAs have identified an amount within the age weighted pupil unit (AWPU) allocation to meet the cost of SENCO time. For example, the average cost of employing a SENCO is identified and then included within the AWPU at a rate sufficient to provide at least one full-time equivalent (FTE) member of staff per 500 pupils. (DfES 2004b: 1.5 (a))

Further activities for SENCOs on remodelling the workforce

The activities below are designed to promote further discussion for SENCOs within their own school and/or within a SENCO Network, on ways forward in meeting the radical changes ahead in relation to re-conceptualising the SENCO role:

- Map and record the time you spend on the key aspects of the SENCO role during a typical term.
- Undertake a benefit analysis exercise of the jobs you have undertaken during that term, highlighting any activities that could have been done by others, and indicating which other staff (support staff, teaching staff) could have undertaken the particular task.
- If you consider the SENCO role is too extensive for one person in your school, in order to meet the *Every Child Matters* agenda, make a list of the barriers that currently prevent you from carrying out your role effectively. Suggest possible solutions in making the SENCO role more manageable, and put forward proposals for improvement to the head teacher and SEN governor, following discussion with your line manager.
- Imagine that you find yourself in the fortunate position to be offered another member of staff from within the school, to become Assistant SENCO. Write a job description for this member of staff, matching the tasks to the knowledge, skills and experience of the colleague concerned.
- Describe the extent of your role for other members of the Change Team. Devise a set of recommendations that would prepare the school for the new SENCO role in an extended school, leading, managing and co-ordinating a multi-disciplinary Inclusion Team of para-professionals from within and outside the school.
- Imagine that the opportunity has arisen for you to become a para-SENCO (peripatetic SENCO), working across a cluster of four schools. Outline how you would be most effectively deployed in this role. Indicate who would be your line manager. What key roles would you undertake in the role? Devise an agreement or contract to clarify and explain your role with the four/partner schools.

Glossary

Assessment for Learning – helps to identify the strengths and weaknesses of individual children. It can be used to track pupil progress, set individual learning targets, tackle underperformance, provide structured feedback to pupils and inform teacher planning. Learners are actively involved in setting the pace and purpose of their learning.

Bureaucracy – administrative activities or other activities which do not relate directly to the delivery of an effective education for pupils, and which would benefit from the use of ICT.

Change – a process to improve practice, introduce new policies and functions, and is a significant alteration in the *status quo*.

Commissioning – a process of changing things, particularly by spending money differently, in order to get better results for people.

Common Assessment Framework – helps all practitioners from services (health, social services and education) to identify the broader needs of a child, using a common and consistent approach to needs assessment for referrals between agencies. It reduces the number of separate assessments for a child.

Contextual value added – compares the progress made by each pupil with the average progress made by similar pupils in similar schools.

Evaluation – concerned with gauging effectiveness, strengths and weaknesses and interpreting how well things are going.

Extended school – a school that provides a range of services and activities often beyond the traditional school day to help meet the needs of its pupils, their families and the wider community.

Inclusion – concerns the quality of children's experience; how they are helped to learn, achieve and participate fully in the life of the school, irrespective of which type of school they attend.

Innovation – refers to an idea or practice which is perceived to be a significant departure from existing practice (something new), and is a social process that takes place through time.

Lead professional – a designated professional who has day-to-day contact with a child, and who co-ordinates service provision for a child or young person, and acts as a gatekeeper for information sharing.

Market – a mechanism whereby individuals or organisations can exchange services which can be both profit-making and non-profit-making from public, private, voluntary and community sectors.

Monitoring – checking progress against targets, looking out for trends in performance indicators and seeing that strategies have been implemented.

National Service Framework – a set of quality standards for health, social care and some education services aimed at reducing inequalities in service provision, in order to improve the lives and health of children and young people.

Para-professional – an individual with some kind of knowledge and training who performs important service delivery activities, and works as part of a multi-disciplinary team across a range of educational settings.

Personalisation – this is where users are active participants in the shaping, development and delivery of education and related services. It creates more involved and responsible users.

Personalised learning – this is about enabling children and young people to achieve the best they can through working in a way that suits them. It embraces every aspect of school life including teaching and learning strategies, ICT, curriculum choice, organisation and timetabling, assessment arrangements and relationships with the local community.

Remodelling – self-directed approach that places the school in control to diagnose its own issues, choose what to work on and to make change happen. It empowers schools to tackle their key issues in a way that reflects their individual circumstances.

Vulnerable – all those children and young people whose lives could be jeopardised unless action is taken to meet their needs and reduce the risk of social exclusion.

Vulnerable children – this covers children and young people in public care (looked after children), children with learning difficulties and disabilities; travellers, asylum seekers, excluded pupils, truants, young offenders, family carers, children living in families where parents have mental illness, alcohol or drug dependency problems; children affected by domestic violence.

Useful Websites

www.cabinet-office.gov.uk/regulation/PublicSector/reports.htm

www.childrenscommissioner.org

www.demos.co.uk

www.dfes.gov.uk/publications/5yearstrategy

www.dh.gov.uk/PolicyAndGuidance/HealthAndSocialCareTopics/ChildrenServices/fs/en

www.diseed.org.uk

www.drc.org.uk/education

www.everychildmatters.gov.uk

www.ncsl.org.uk/lftm

www.ofsted.gov.uk/publications

www.ofsted.gov.uk/documents/schooltraining/senimslic.pdf

www.remodelling.org

www.standards.dfes.gov.uk/innovation-unit

www.teachernet.gov.uk/senexpenditure

www.teachernet.gov.uk/_doc/7373/Autism.pdf

References and Further Reading

Bond, K. and Waterhouse, J. (2005) *Building New Relationships in a Networked Landscape*. NCSL Conference. London: National College for School Leadership.

Cole, B. (2005) *Inclusion, SENCOs and the Law. SENCO Update*, **63**, 6–7. London: Optimus Publishing.

Collarbone, P. (2005) *Innovation and the Remodelling School*. NCSL Conference. London: National College for School Leadership.

DfEE (1998) Circular 2/98: *Reducing the Bureaucratic Burden on Teachers*. London: Department for Education and Employment.

DfES (2001a) Teachers' Standards Framework. London: Department for Education and Skills.

DfES (2001b) Special Educational Needs Code of Practice. London: Department for Education and Skills.

DfES (2002) *An Introduction to Extended Schools: Providing Opportunities and Services for All*. London: Department for Education and Skills.

DfES (2003a) *Every Child Matters*. London: Department for Education and Skills.

DfES (2003b) *Every Child Matters* (Summary). London: Department for Education and Skills.

DfES (2003c) *Making a Difference: A Guide for Special Educational Needs (SEN) Governors*. London: Department for Education and Skills.

DfES (2003d) *Bureaucracy Cutting Tool Kit*. London: Department for Education and Skills.

DfES (2004a) *Removing Barriers to Achievement. The Government's Strategy for SEN*. London: Department for Education and Skills.

DfES (2004b) *The Management of SEN Expenditure*. London: Department for Education and Skills.

DfES (2004c) *School Profile Consultation*. London: Department for Education and Skills.

DfES (2004d) *Five Year Strategy for Children and Learners*. London: Department for Education and Skills.

DfES/OFSTED (2004e) *A New Relationship with Schools: Improving Performance through School Self-Evaluation*. London: Department for Education and Skills/Office for Standards in Education.

DfES (2004f) *Every Child Matters: Next Steps*. London: Department for Education and Skills.

DfES (2004g) *Every Child Matters – Outcomes Framework*. London: Department for Education and Skills.

DfES (2004h) *Guidance for Schools on Higher Level Teaching Assistant Roles for School Support Staff*. London: Department for Education and Skills.

DfES (2004j) *National Standards for Headteachers*. London: Department for Education and Skills.

DfES (2004k) *A Ten Year Strategy for Childcare*. London: Department for Education and Skills.

DfES (2004m) *Every Child Matters: Change for Children in Schools*. London: Department for Education and Skills.

DfES (2004n) *Developing the Role of School Support Staff – What the National Agreement Means for You*. London: Department for Education and Skills.

DfES (2004p) *A National Conversation about Personalised Learning*. London: Department for Education and Skills.

DfES (2004q) *Picture This! Planning for Personalisation*. London: Department for Education and Skills.

DfES (2005a) *Leading on Inclusion. National Primary Strategy*. London: Department for Education and Skills.

DfES (2005b) *Promoting Inclusion and Tackling Underperformance. Maximising Progress: Ensuring the Attainment of Pupils with SEN*. Key Stage 3 National Strategy. London: Department for Education and Skills.

DfES/Cabinet Office RIU (2004) *Special Educational Needs – Bureaucracy Project Summary Report*. London: Department for Education and Skills/Cabinet Office Regulatory Impact Unit.

DfES/DH (2004a) *National Service Framework for Children, Young People and Maternity Services – Executive Summary*. London: Department for Education and Skills/Department of Health.

DfES/DH (2004b) *National Service Framework for Children, Young People and Maternity Services – Disabled Children and Young People with Complex Health Needs*. London: Department for Education and Skills/Department of Health.

DfES/DH (2004c) *National Service Framework for Children, Young People and Maternity Services – Autism Spectrum Disorders*. London: Department for Education and Skills/Department of Health.

DfES/OFSTED (2005) *A New Relationship with Schools: Next Steps*. London: Department for Education and Skills/Office for Standards in Education.

Farrar, M. and Walker, L. (2005) *Seizing Success. New Relationships across Sectors*. NCSL Conference. London: National College for School Leadership.

Gross, J. and White, A. (2003) *Special Educational Needs and School Improvement. Practical Strategies for Raising Standards*. London: David Fulton Publishers.

Hargreaves, D. (2003) *Working Laterally: How Innovation Networks Make an Education Epidemic*. London: Department for Education and Skills.

Lancashire County Council (2002) *Performance Indicators for Value Added Target Setting* (Rev. edn). Preston: Lancashire Professional Development Service.

Leadbetter, C. (2004) *Learning about Personalisation: How Can We Put the Learner at the Heart of the Education System?* London: Department for Education and Skills.

Lindsey, J.D. (1983) 'Paraprofessionals in learning disabilities'. *Journal of Learning Disabilities*, **16**(8).

NUT (2004) *Special Educational Needs Co-ordinators and the Revised Code of Practice: An NUT Survey*. London: National Union of Teachers.

OECD (2003) *Education Policy Analysis* (2003 edition). London: Organisation for Economic Co-operation and Development.

OFSTED (2004a) *Special Educational Needs and Disability: Towards Inclusive Schools*. London: Office for Standards in Education.

OFSTED (2004b) *Guidance for Inspectors of Schools. Conducting the Inspection*. London: Office for Standards in Education.

OFSTED (2005a) *Self-Evaluation Form for Secondary Schools*. London: Office for Standards in Education.

OFSTED (2005b) Annual Report of Her Majesty's Chief Inspector of Schools: *Standards and Quality in Education 2003/2004*. London: Office for Standards in Education.

OFSTED (2005c) *Every Child Matters Framework for the Inspection of Schools in England from September 2005*. London: Office for Standards in Education.

PCW (2004) *Scoping the Market for Children's Services. Report for the Department for Education and Skills*. London: PriceWaterhouseCoopers.

Robertson, C. (2004) 'Time to grasp the nettle?' *SENCO Update*, **54**. London: Optimus Publishing.

TTA (1998) *National Standards for Special Educational Needs Coordinators*. London: Teacher Training Agency.

Index